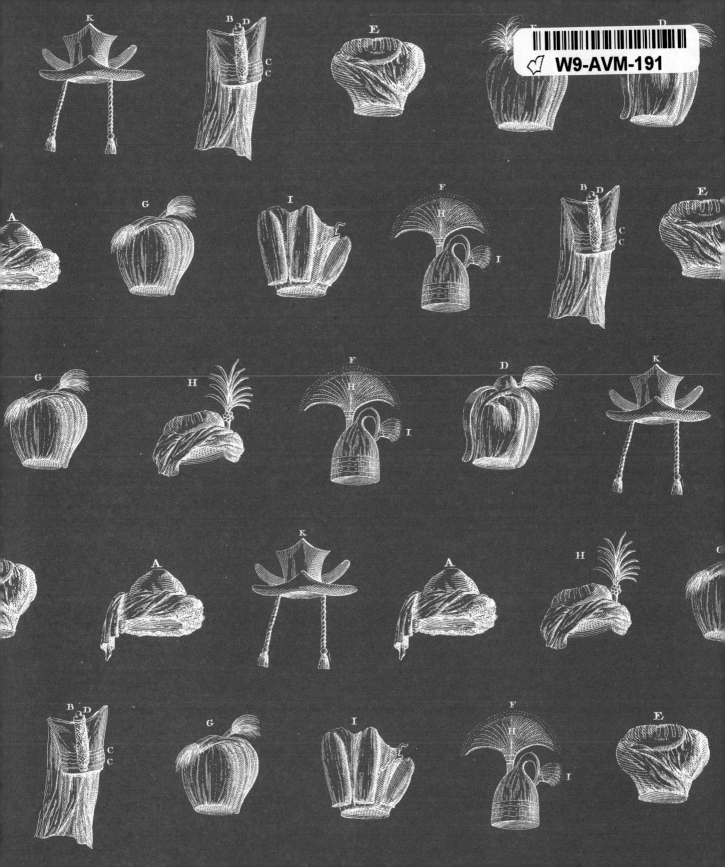

Turkish Delights

Turkish Delights

Philippa Scott

With 167 illustrations, 156 in color

 Thames & Hudson

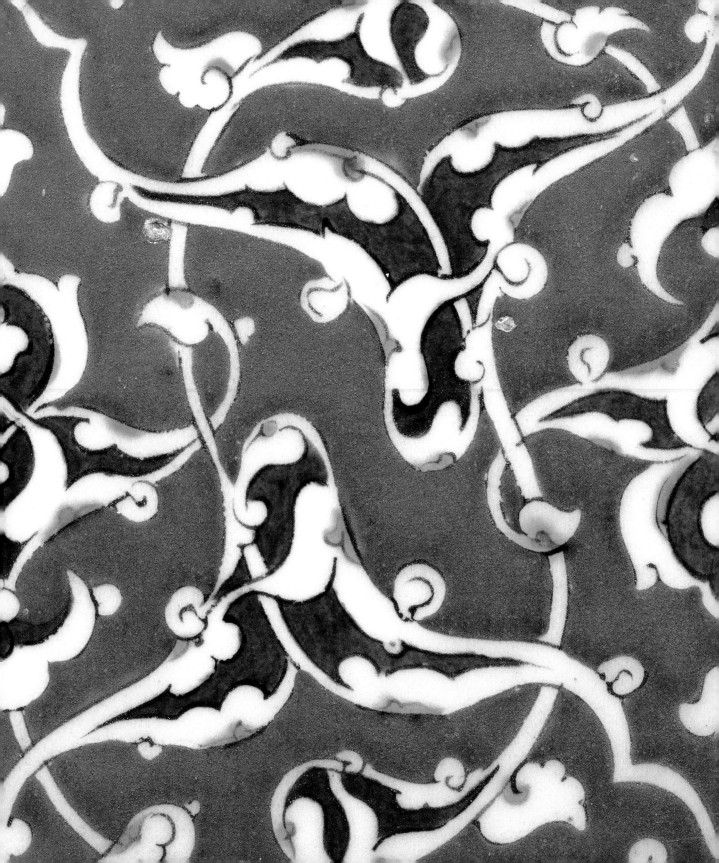

To the Memory of Robert Tewdwr-Moss

ENDPAPERS: from L. F. Marsigli, *Stato Militare dell' Imperio Ottomanno*, The Hague, 1732.
PAGE 3: Arab Hall, Leighton House, London; lined with Ottoman tiles.
PAGE 4: *Mehmet II, the Conqueror*, by Siblizade Ahmed, late 15th century; Topkapi Sarayi Library, Istanbul.
PAGE 5: View of Constantinople, 1536; University Library, Istanbul.
PAGE 6: Detail from *The Triumph of St George*, by Vittore Carpaccio, 1504–6; Scuola di Giorgio, Venice.
PAGE 7: Ceremonial kaftan of Sultan Bayezid II (1481–1512), silk and gold lampas woven in the Imperial *ateliers* in Bursa; Topkapi Sarayi Museum, Istanbul.
PAGE 8: Iznik border tile with repeating arabesque pattern, second half of the 16th century; private collection.
PAGE 9: Iznik tiles with tulips, hyacinths and sprays of prunus blossom, *c.* 1560; ex-author's collection.
PAGES 10–11: *Tughra* (ceremonial signature), detail, of Suleyman the Magnificent (1520–66); Topkapi Sarayi Museum, Istanbul.

Picture Research: Georgina Bruckner

© 2001 Philippa Scott
Design and layout © 2001 Thames & Hudson Ltd, London

First published in the United States of America in hardcover in 2001 by Thames & Hudson Inc., 500 Fifth Avenue, New York, New York 10110

Library of Congress Catalog Card Number 00-107616
ISBN 0-500-51037-7

Printed and bound in Singapore by C. S. Graphics

CONTENTS

INTRODUCTION

Without the contributions and influence of the Ottoman Turks, life would be different and diminished. For centuries Western art and culture have been enriched and refined in many ways which today we take for granted. There are the obvious pleasures: Turkish Delight, Turkish slippers, Turkish cigarettes. The first travellers to experience the Turkish bath described Turkish towelling with enthusiasm, and in Victorian Britain alone some six hundred Turkish baths were built, due partly to a Scottish diplomat's book written after his first-hand experience in Constantinople.

Other Ottoman antecedents include the tulip, coffee, the croissant, the sorbet, the sash; words like kiosk, ottoman, sofa, divan. Initially all carpets were called Turkish because they were traded and exported from there. Certain carpet designs are known today by the names of particular artists, such as Lotto, who used them as studio props to signify a sitter's prestige. European-made copies were simply, 'Turkeyeworke'.

The first longhaired cats brought to the West were all 'Turkish' – breeders in the nineteenth century created the modern Persian cat. Mohair comes from the Angora, or Ankara goat, even today bred successfully in only five places worldwide. The Turks, not the Florentines, invented paper marbling, originally 'Turkey paper'. Ottoman techniques of

LEFT: Imaginary portrait of Samson Rowlie; from a manuscript, Bodleian Library, Oxford, 1588. The son of a Bristol merchant, Rowlie was captured by Algerian corsairs. By 1586 he was Hasan Aga, a Muslim and eunuch, and Treasurer to the Bey of Algiers (Algiers was in the Ottoman Empire). OPPOSITE: Suleyman the Magnificent, detail from a painting by Nigari, *c.* 1560; Topkapi Sarayi Museum, Istanbul. The Ottoman Golden Era was the reign of Suleyman the Magnificent (1520–66), known as *Kanuni* (the Lawgiver). OVERLEAF: Detail of Melchior Lorichs' drawing, *Long View of Constantinople*, 1559; Leiden University Library. Lorichs joined the entourage of the Ambassador of the Holy Roman Empire to the court of Suleyman.

shagreen (sharkskin), and 'carpet patterns' for tooled leather bindings spread rapidly via Venice. Europe's craze for silhouette portraiture had a Turkish origin, as did Boulle marquetry in tortoiseshell and brass. In his *Memoirs,* Benvenuto Cellini, the leading sculptor and goldsmith of the sixteenth century, confessed that the workmanship of a Turkish dagger challenged him to try damascening (a gold and silver pattern inlaid in steel). After the second Siege of Vienna in 1683, country houses all over Europe featured Turkish tents in landscape designs, and built Turkish 'smoking rooms'. Was Lewis Carroll inspired by tales of Constantinople's fortune-telling white rabbits? The Ottoman 'language of flowers' became a Western craze, and lingers still in greeting cards and St Valentine's Day bouquets. Smallpox inoculation by 'engrafting' predated Edward Jenner's injection, and was introduced from Turkey in the early eighteenth century by Lady Mary Wortley Montagu. Lady Mary's observations of women's dress and undress inspired Ingres' fantasized scenes of Turkish baths, and many subsequent painters with overheated imagination. Matisse wrote of Rembrandt's Biblical scenes

'*avec de vraies turqueries de bazar*', and Rembrandt's *Portrait of a Turk* was one of Catherine the Great's first purchases for the Winter Palace. From the late nineteenth century, William Morris, William de Morgan, Cantagalli, Joseph-Théodore Deck, Louis Tiffany, Mariano Fortuny, and many others copied and adapted Ottoman designs. Literature, theatre and opera featured Ottoman themes, composers incorporated Eastern flourishes and janissary percussion and rhythms. Before designing St Paul's dome, Christopher Wren studied Ottoman architecture. 'Turkey Red' was the most desirable dye, an elusive secret derived from Anatolian madder. The turkey, the large American bird with its crimson head and wattle, is named for this dye. All in all, this is a rich inheritance.

OPPOSITE: *Seated Scribe*, though attributed to Gentile Bellini, it belongs to a series of such portraits by Persian, Mughal and Turkish artists, 16th century; Isabella Stewart Gardner Museum, Boston. ABOVE: *Reception of the Ambassadors*, artist unknown, *c.* 1500; Louvre, Paris. Although earlier artists showed Oriental figures in imaginary settings, this is the first European painting to show a recognizable Oriental setting, in this case Damascus. From 1517, Mamluk Egypt and Syria were part of the Ottoman Empire. The seated figure at the mosque entrance wears the distinctive Mamluk *al-naura* (waterwheel) turban.

Constantinople was brutally sacked by the Fourth Crusade in 1204, when Christian slaughtered Christian in the name of God but with the purpose of booty. The proud bronze horses above St Mark's Square in Venice were part of this plunder.

18

As Ottoman power increased, subsequent Byzantine emperors repeatedly petitioned Christian powers for help and reinforcements. No help came. When Constantinople fell to the Turks, as was inevitable, there was outcry throughout Christendom; the clamour of hypocrisy. The first tickets that were ever issued were Indulgences – slips of paper promising remission of the punishment due to sin after absolution – in other words, tickets to Heaven. These were granted in 1454 by Pope Nicholas V to those who gave money to help the campaign against the Ottoman Turks. Too little, too late. Already, on 29 May 1453, after several months' siege, Ottoman troops had broken through the great wall of Constantinople. Twenty-two-year-old Sultan Mehmet II, henceforth known as 'Fatih', the Conqueror, rode to the mother church of Eastern Christendom, Haghia Sophia (Divine Wisdom). Dismounting, he bent to pick up a handful of earth which he poured over his turban as an act of humility before God. He surveyed Constantinople from the roof of the great church and wandered amid the ruins of Byzantine palaces. Mindful of life's impermanence, he quietly recited the lines of the poet-philosopher Sa'adi:

THE SPIDER WEAVES THE CURTAINS IN THE PALACE OF CHOSROES,
THE OWL CALLS THE WATCHES IN AFRASYAB'S TOWERS.

Mehmet knew that trade meant wealth, and that the city needed populating and provisioning. He encouraged foreign merchants, expanded trading alliances and founded the covered Grand Bazaar. His interests were wide-ranging. He commissioned translations of Greek and Latin texts, and collected maps for the library of his new palace. In 1479, when peace was agreed after sixteen years of war with Venice, Mehmet asked the Doge to send 'a good painter' to Constantinople. In due course, the Doge's official artist, Gentile Bellini, arrived, and he stayed for over a year to paint portraits of the 'falcon-nosed' Sultan and his court.

The new Turkish city developed around the mosque complexes built by the Sultan and his viziers, and continued under his successors. Transfused with Ottoman energy, Constantinople began a new, vigorous life, and became the only truly cosmopolitan city in the world, an important diplomatic capital and training-ground of future foreign ministers. Under succeeding Sultans, the Ottoman Empire expanded to rule eastern Europe, western Asia, most of the Maghreb (north-west Africa), and held together lands with very different political traditions, many ethnic groups, and various religious communities. This remained so until the fall of the Ottoman Empire. In 1923, as part of Mustafa Kemal Ataturk's modernization plans for the Republic of Turkey, Ankara became the capital and first city of the new Turkish state. Yet, to the visitor this ancient capital remains the heart of the country. The city's present name, Istanbul (Stamboul), derives from the Greek meaning in, or to, the city. To the first Ottomans it was the Red Apple, the most desirable city on earth. Built on seven hills, it stretches along both Asian and European shores of the Bosphorus. No city in the world better symbolizes the dynamics of East and West, and their irresistible mutual attraction.

THE TURBAN

The Muslim covered his head as a sign of respect for God, and the turban's practical shape, without a brim, did not interfere with his obeisances in prayer. The typically Ottoman turban consisted of fine white muslin-weave cotton, or silk and cotton, wound round a vertically ribbed crimson velvet cap, the *taj*, which had been introduced by Mehmet the Conqueror, and is shown in portraits of the Sultan. Turbans (*kavuk*) varied according to status and rank, and punishment or disgrace included the removal of one's turban. The turban was made by sewing many layers of stuffed cloth into shape, and, once assembled, it was never dismantled. At night the turban was placed in a niche, or on a special stand called a *kavukluk*. When not in use, a square embroidered wrapping cloth, *bohça*, covered the turban.

It can be seen from Carpaccio's paintings that, like some other artists, he clearly had the opportunity to study at first hand details of dress worn by the Turks and the Arabs who came to Venice in the early fifteenth century. Western diplomats to Constantinople were often accompanied by artists – besides painting embassy scenes, they, like the early travellers, also recorded their impressions in books illustrated by engravings of Ottoman costumes; Samuel Pepys, for example, owned a series of de Chapelle's *Turkish Women* prints.

Anthony Jenkinson was the first Briton to record a visit to the Ottoman Empire. He travelled there in 1553, and described Suleyman the Magnificent in this way: '…and upon his head a goodly white tuck, containing in length by estimation fifteene yards, which was of silke and linen woven together

OPPOSITE: The Sultan's
Carrier of Turbans, detail from
a Turkish miniature, 18th century;
Bibliothèque National, Paris.
LEFT: Nasreddin Hodja, a favourite
'wise idiot' character in popular
moralistic folk tales, Turkish
miniature, 18th century; Topkapi
Sarayi Museum, Istanbul.
ABOVE: Turban stand, *kavukluk*,
18th century; private collection.
BELOW: Portrait of Ahmet III
(reigned 1703–30), with the Crown
Prince, painted by the court artist
Levni; Topkapi Sarayi Museum,
Istanbul. Ahmet's turban, with three
aigrettes, is higher than earlier styles.

OPPOSITE ABOVE, CENTRE
BELOW AND LEFT: Three details
from *The Legend of St George* series,
by Vittore Carpaccio, *c.* 1504–6;
Scuola S. Giorgio, Venice. These
show a turban wrapped round a
15th-century *taj* (the vertically ribbed
crimson velvet cap), and also men
wearing the broad flattened turban
of the religious body, the *ulema*.
CENTRE ABOVE: Hayrettin Pasha,
painted by the court artist Nigari,
c. 1560; Topkapi Sarayi Museum,
Istanbul. Nicknamed Barbarossa
for the red beard of his youth, the
Sultan's Admiral made the Turkish
navy into the strongest fleet in
the Mediterranean.
OPPOSITE BELOW: *Man in a
Red Turban,* 1433, by Jan Van Eyck;
National Gallery, London. This
shows a European impression
of a turban, clumsily wrapped,
of the desirable 'Turkey Red',
a secret recipe and speciality
of Ottoman dyers.
ABOVE: Detail from a miniature
illustrating the *Nusretname*
(the chronicles of Nusret),
1582, British Library, London.

resembling something Callicut cloth, but is much more fine and riche, and in the toppe of his crowne a little pinnacle of white ostrich feathers….'

To 'take the turban' or, 'to turn Turk', signified a European who adopted Islam. Then in the seventeenth and eighteenth centuries, when wigs were the fashion, turbans for men became established as Western informal wear when the wig was off. In 1666 Pepys visited Sir Philip Howard, whose 'undress' of Turkish turban and nightrobe made a great impression on the diarist. Without the assistance of a servant whose specific duty was the assembly and care of his master's turban, Western versions often tended to be the precariously tied attempts that feature in such paintings as Van Eyck's *Man in a Red Turban*. Later this was replaced by a type of small Turkish cap, often embroidered velvet, worn with a smoking jacket, again a form of

casual attire based on the notional East, for in Turkey this type of cap was in fact worn by women, not men, and wound around with an embroidered scarf. The *nargileh*-smoking caterpillar encountered by Carroll's Alice on her adventures in Wonderland is usually drawn wearing a little Turkish cap.

When Ahmet I dedicated the Sultan Ahmet mosque, the 'Blue Mosque', in 1616, it is said that, as a gesture of

OPPOSITE AND LEFT:
Marble tombstones topped with
carved turbans and headgear;
Eyup Cemetery, Istanbul.
ABOVE: Calligraphy in the shape
of a Sufi Dervish hat, Topkapi Sarayi
Museum, Istanbul. Originally brightly
painted, the different marble turbans
denoted rank – the tombstones of
important women were carved with
flowers instead. When the turban
was banned in 1829, tombstones were
topped by a stone fez. Muslim cemeteries,
where the gravestones are scattered
as irregularly as the flowers and shrubs
planted there, were popular for picnics
and illicit romantic trysts. The oldest
Turkish cemetery in Istanbul, dating
back to 1452, is at Rumeli Hisari,
Mehmet II's fortress on the Bosphorus.
There used to be a dervish *tekke*,
meeting house, below the fortress,
and many saints were buried there.
Their tombstones are topped by the
characteristic dervish headdress and
turban. Sufis take their name from *suf*,
wool, a reference to their clothes and
their distinctive tall felt hat. Best
known in the West are the Mevlevi
order, the so-called 'whirling dervishes'.

humility, he wore a turban shaped like the foot of the Prophet Mohammad. *Hajjis*, those who had completed the pilgrimage to Mecca, were entitled to a green turban. Holy men wore black robes and wound their turbans round a skull cap so that they were wider and flatter. A headdress peculiar to the Janissaries symbolized the white or red sleeve of the Bektasis (a Sufi order), folded high above the brow to hang down their necks. This was varied by adding ornaments and plumes. Among the military, red headwear signified that the wearer was Turkish by birth and Muslim by faith, and slave troops were identified by their white caps.

On occasions, or according to protocol or individual taste, turbans were decorated with jewels or a feathered aigrette. In response to overtures from Henri III of France, Mehmet the Conqueror requested 'a very small striking clock, oval in shape, to wear in the turban', and the same for a favourite official. Alas, the Sultan was to be disappointed. The French King felt this would be too costly a diplomatic gift.

In Turkey, the funerary stelae of the women were decorated in low relief with flowers, but those of the men were surmounted by a stone headdress as worn by the deceased in life. Tombstones topped by a turban date from before 1829. After this, they were carved with a fez. Like the Stambouli, or frock coat, the fez was introduced by Mahmud II as one of his modernizations. Initially, both fashions met fierce opposition. The effect on turban-makers and the textile trade in general was devastating, although tassel-makers saw their profits soar, for fez tassels had to be replaced at least once a year. Suddenly the streets

BACKGROUND: Fez and jewelled aigrette of Sultan Abdulmecit, 19th century; Topkapi Sarayi Treasury.
OPPOSITE LEFT: Schéhérezade, by George Barbier, from the fashion journal *Modes et manières d'aujourd'hui*, 1914.
OPPOSITE RIGHT: Fashion plate, by George Barbier, 1919.
OPPOSITE BELOW: Turkish Janissary, etching by Master L. D., Lyons, 1568. George Barbier was an influential designer and illustrator, closely associated with Paul Poiret. Though Poiret denied that he was influenced by the dramatic costumes of the Ballet Russes, who first performed in Paris in 1909, his designs, were, all the same , daringly different from the formal silhouette and corseted dresses of the period. Turbans, aigrettes and harem pants featured in his 1909 collection.

of Istanbul were full of little boys offering to comb tassels for a small consideration. Julia Pardoe in her *Beauties of the Bosphorus* complained that from a distance a group of Turks in their red fezzes looked like a field of poppies. Only the clergy were permitted to retain the distinctive long robes and turbans. Less than a hundred years later, in 1925, the fez in turn was outlawed by Ataturk's far-reaching reforms.

Both the turban and its jewelled or feathered aigrettes became fashionable in Western women's wear, still making an appearance on international catwalks whenever taste returns to Oriental mode. Two influential designers and illustrators of the early twentieth century were the Russian Erté and the French George Barbier, both of whom were associated with the designer Paul Poiret. In 1909 Poiret featured turbans, aigrettes, tunics and harem pants, daringly different and exotic garments, provoking keen interest when seen on stage in the Ballets Russes, which the impresario Sergei Diaghilev first introduced to an amazed Parisian audience in 1909 – the vivid Central Asian silk costumes were a contrast to the sweet-pea colours of the fashion of the time. From 1910 to 1920 the turban became a popular style, preconstructed by milliners into the shape now so familiar. It enjoyed a resurgence in the 1930s, then again in the 1960s and the 1980s, and is now a classic.

TULIPS AND POMEGRANATES

FOOTMAN, POUR ME SOME WINE, FOR ONE DAY THE TULIP GARDEN WILL BE DESTROYED;
AUTUMN WILL COME, AND THE SPRING SEASON WILL BE NO MORE.

This reflective couplet by Mehmet the Conqueror reveals the special affection that the Ottomans held for tulips. The Turks created many different styles of garden – the best loved were those that were informally planted, meandering, scented, and with water and trees – but a garden was not a garden unless there were tulips. George Sandys, travelling in Turkey in the early seventeenth century, wrote: 'You cannot stirre abroad but you shall be presented by the dervishes and janizaries with tulips and trifles.'

The first Western travellers marvelled that the Ottomans so loved these 'red lilies' that they often wore a single tulip in their turbans, like a plumed aigrette. To the Turks they are *lâle*, written with the same Arabic letters as 'Allah', and therefore often used as a religious symbol. The famous Iznik tiles of the Rustem Pasha mosque boast Istanbul's most spectacular banks of tulips, forty-one varieties, real and imaginary, but a visitor to the baroque Lâleli mosque, will find its walls covered in rare marble and semi-precious stones, and tulips only in its name. A delight to poets, *lâle* rhymes with *piyale*, wine glass.

The introduction of the tulip to the West resulted in Dutch 'Tulip Fever', when bulbs changed hands for huge sums. Seventeenth-century Dutch flower paintings show the streaked

OPPOSITE: The Sultan's favourite holding a tulip, by Levni, Ahmet III's court painter, 18th century; Topkapi Sarayi Museum, Istanbul.

LEFT: A scene from a tulip celebration, Turkish miniature, 17th century; Topkapi Sarayi, Istanbul.

ABOVE: Delft tulip vases, 17th century; Royal Palace of Het Loo, Apeldoorn, Netherlands. With the advent of Dutch Tulip Fever, vases were created to display these treasured flowers, a single stem inserted into each opening. Turbanned Turk's heads were popular, as were pyramid forms.

BELOW: Page from *Lâle Memuasi*, Turkish Tulip Album, 1725.

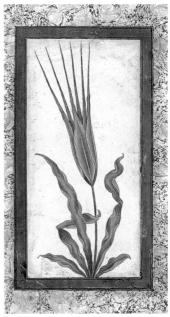

and parrot-petalled flowers developed by bulb-growers once they had identified and manipulated the virus, transmitted by aphids, which caused the colours to break. Alexandre Dumas's novel *The Black Tulip* recalls the intensity of Dutch tulip-mania. The Ottomans also genetically modified bulbs, but their preference speci-fied dagger-shaped flowers tapering to long narrow petals. The closest surviving relative to these is *Tulipa acuminata.* I have grown this bulb; the spaghetti-thin petals, yellow streaked and tipped with scarlet, twist and turn, and each day it looks more wonderfully crazed.

The Ottomans preferred a single bloom in a narrow necked vase, *lâledan*, which Dutch ceramicists elaborated into pyramid or portrait vases. In the Language of Flowers, originally a Turkish affectation, the gift of a red tulip conveys, 'I am on fire from your beauty,' and by its black base that the lover's heart is burned to coal. A thread of silk says, 'I love you with rapture.' Raptures of tulips bloom in Ottoman silks, ceramics, metal, stone and wood. Suleyman the Magnificent's campaign armour was embossed with a single glorious tulip, twenty-two centimetres, nine inches, long, and his turban helmet was crowned with tulips made of gold and

OPPOSITE: A lustrous silk woven in Bursa, 17th century; Francesca Galloway, London.
ABOVE LEFT: Parade shield, cane whipped with silk thread, 16th century; Topkapi Sarayi Museum, Istanbul.
BELOW LEFT: Ceremonial kaftan of Suleyman the Magnificent, an Italian version of a Bursa silk and gold velvet, 16th century; and ceremonial kaftan of Suleyman III, appliquéd lamé on satin, 17th century. Both Topkapi Sarayi Museum, Istanbul.
OVERLEAF FROM LEFT: Iznik tiles; Rustem Pasha Mosque, Istanbul, 1561. Wallpaper design by William Morris, late 19th century, Victoria & Albert Museum, London. Printed velvet by Fortuny, *c.* 1930, after a 16th-century Ottoman silk. Tulip (detail), from a 16th-century Ottoman silk; Musée Historique des Tissus, Lyons.

set with jewels. In one painting in the 1582 *Sûrname* album, depicting celebrations for the circumcision of Sultan Murad III's heir, a procession of turbanned Turks carries towering pagodas, each resplendent with red tulips. Ahmet III commissioned the Fruit Room in the Topkapi Sarayi, an intimate dining-space painted with dishes of fruits and vases of his favourite flowers. This Sultan, whose rule is known as *Lâle Devri*, the Tulip Reign, instituted an annual festival to celebrate the blossoming of his obsession. For three days surrounding the first full moon in April, the Topkapi gardens were transformed into fairyland with displays of tulips, coloured lanterns, caged nightingales, music and dancers, and tortoises with candles stuck to their shells. One evening the women of the harem organized a mock bazaar; naturally the Sultan was their only client. The Flower Market still flourishes next to the the Yeni Çamii (New Mosque), where Ahmet, the Tulip King, was buried.

The Sultans ate from Chinese porcelain, and the Topkapi houses the largest collection of Chinese ceramics outside China. Ottoman artists freely incorporated Chinese cloudbands and lotus palmettes with the flowers of Anatolia. The oldest Ottoman motifs, from pre-Islamic times, are celestial; radiant sun, star, crescent moon. Moving west, they adopted Near East motifs: the distinctive arabesque (*rumi*), Tree of Life, centifolia rosette, pine-cone, cypress and pomegranate.

Pomegranates, representing fertility, have long been associated with the Near Eastern Great Goddess in all her forms. In some Ottoman embroideries of the seventeenth century and later, the image of the pomegranate is so distorted that it appears to explode. If left to dry on the branch, pomegranates will indeed eventually burst, scattering their seeds.

In Turkey, Italy and Spain in the fourteenth, fifteenth and sixteenth centuries, technical advances produced velvets enriched with complex gold brocading and bouclé. Travelling west, a version of pomegranate palmettes became the favourite velvet motif in Spain and Italy, whereas the Ottomans preferred carnation palmettes. A form similar to this is found on *kilims*, and current research suggests that this design can be traced to the Neolithic peoples of Anatolia. The pomegranate symbolizes the world, and its seeds represent humanity. A decorative motif, a royal design reserved for the Ottoman court, it was never depicted on trousers or slippers.

Vying with the tulip is the *çintamani*, originally a Buddhist symbol, and later adopted as the blazon of the Timurid dynasty. Often combined with wavy lines, and suggestive of leopard and tiger skins, the dots, like closed crescents, are also frequently included in floral patterns.

OPPOSITE: Detail from 17th-century Ottoman embroidery, silk on linen.
ABOVE: Pomegranate, detail from an Ottoman embroidered *bohça* (wrapping cloth), 18th century; private collection.
BELOW: Frieze of Russian tiles, pomegranate design, imitating the Ottoman style, 1667; St George of Neo-Cesarea Church, Moscow. Catherine the Great's dream, shared by most Greeks in the Ottoman Empire, was to make Constantinople once more the capital of the Eastern Christian Church.

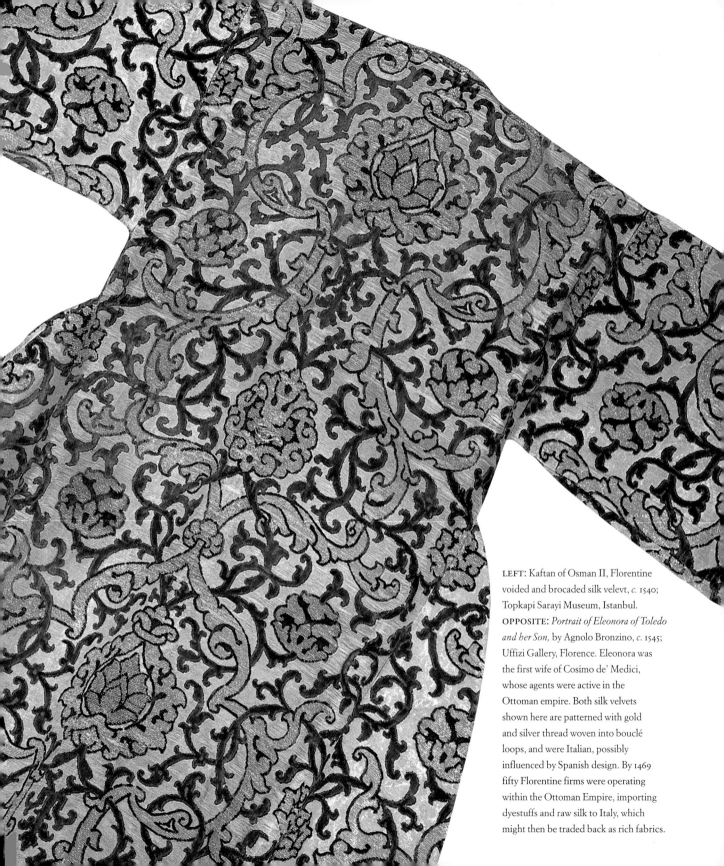

LEFT: Kaftan of Osman II, Florentine voided and brocaded silk velevt, *c. 1540;* Topkapi Sarayi Museum, Istanbul. OPPOSITE: *Portrait of Eleonora of Toledo and her Son,* by Agnolo Bronzino, *c. 1545;* Uffizi Gallery, Florence. Eleonora was the first wife of Cosimo de' Medici, whose agents were active in the Ottoman empire. Both silk velvets shown here are patterned with gold and silver thread woven into bouclé loops, and were Italian, possibly influenced by Spanish design. By 1469 fifty Florentine firms were operating within the Ottoman Empire, importing dyestuffs and raw silk to Italy, which might then be traded back as rich fabrics.

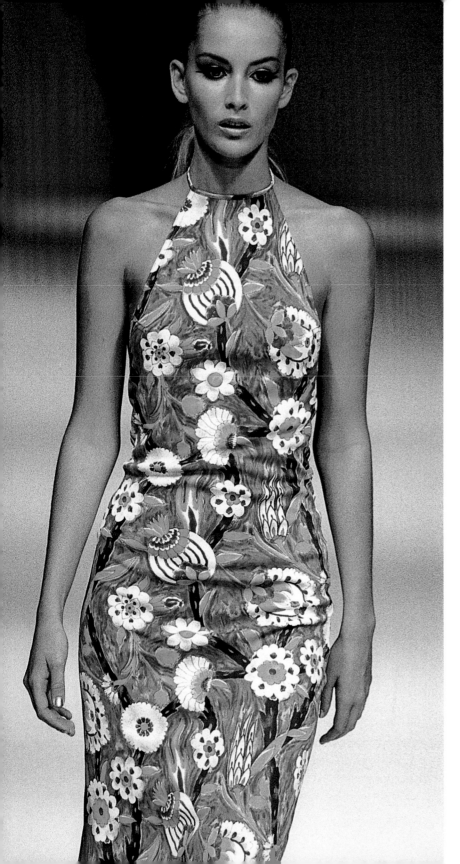

OPPOSITE: Iznik tile with lotus palmettes, *saz* leaves (curved plumey leaves named for the calligrapher's reed pen), prunus blossoms, part of a large panel, end of the 16th century; Rustem Pasha Mosque, Istanbul.
THIS PAGE: Silk dress, designed by Rifat Ozbek, Spring/Summer Collection 1994. The fabric chosen by this London-based Turkish couturier closely reflects the pattern and colours of the Iznik tiles. Ozbek's designs frequently take inspiration from Ottoman opulence and his own Turkish heritage. His first major collection was shown in Paris in 1994 and featured designs derived from 16th-century court fashions.

MAGIC CARPETS

There are many stories about magic flying carpets, and there are even more theories. One story describes a certain Byzantine Emperor whose throne rose in the air when a supplicant approached. Legend does not relate whether the throne depended on a throne carpet for its elevation, but if the carpet beneath the throne was knotted, one might safely hazard a guess that it was woven by Turkish magic and Turkish fingers.

The oldest carpet so far discovered by archaeologists was preserved in permafrost in a rich Scythian grave in the Altai Mountains of far Siberia. It was woven some time around 500 BC, and displays sophistication and already long-established skill. Rug-weaving is very extravagant with material, and demands the ready availability of wool. Knotted carpets and geometric patterns are found all along the Turks' route as they grazed their flocks from the Central Asian heartlands to Turkey, where they eventually settled. However, *kilims* and various supplementary thread flatweaves had been woven in Anatolia long before the arrival of the Turks, and some of the indigenous patterns have been traced to Neolithic times.

OPPOSITE: Detail from the *Legend of St George* series, by Vittore Carpaccio, 1504–6, Scuola de S. Giorgio, Venice. Citizens displayed their wealth by hanging Turkish rugs over their balconies like banners. **LEFT:** Silk Hereke rug, late 19th/early 20th century. The designers of the Hereke *atelier* freely cannibalized patterns and motifs from many sources, and the results can be surprising. State-owned today, Hereke was initially set up in the mid-19th century by a pair of brothers, the Dadyans, to produce furnishing and other textiles for the Ottoman court. Hereke silks can be finely woven, but never as fine as those signed by one of the best Armenian master weavers from the Kum Kapi workshops in Istanbul, which were also set up in the mid-19th century.

LEFT: Ushak carpet (details), 16th century, Phoenix Collection. Although Lorenzo Lotto shows various carpet designs in his paintings, his name has become associated with the geometric foliate trellis shown here. We know that he owned at least one rug – his account books record his pawning a carpet, but not its pattern.

BELOW LEFT: Detail from *Family Group*, 16th century, by Lorenzo Lotto, National Gallery, London. The artist has altered the colour scheme and has here made the typical field with yellow tracery red on red for dramatic effect.

OPPOSITE: 'Memling' carpet (detail), Ushak, 16th century; Hungarian Museum of Applied Arts, Budapest. *Virgin and Child* by Hans Memling, 15th century, Louvre, Paris. Memling painted several carpets of the 'Holbein' type, but his name has become associated with a field pattern of hooked medallions, known as 'Memling guls'. These appear on Turkish, Caucasian and Kurdish rugs.

Turkish carpets have been imported into Europe since the fourteenth century or even earlier. Their patterns included stylized birds or animals within octagons, and two such carpets were found in churches, one in Sweden and one in Italy; in recent years another came to light in a ransacked Tibetan monastery, and is now a star exhibit in an American museum. Similar rugs appear in many fourteenth- and fifteenth-century paintings of the Madonna and Child. The fourteenth-century Pope Benedict XII always kept a favourite carpet with him – patterned with large spotted birds in octagons, the carpet features in a fresco in the Palais des Papes in Avignon.

During the sixteenth and seventeenth centuries, Europe's hunger for these luxury goods escalated. In 1520 Cardinal Wolsey ordered sixty Turkish carpets through the Signory of Venice, which controlled the trade. Henry VIII of England owned some four hundred, and was painted by Eworth and Holbein standing proudly on different medallion Ushaks. Fine carpets were symbols of status, usually displayed on a table, too precious for the floor. They were made in *ateliers* capable of fulfilling court and other major commissions. Ushak patterns were copied in Europe either by needlework or knotting, and known as 'Turkeyeworke'. The first prayer rugs to reach the West were called muskey or musket rugs, from the word 'mosque'. Certain patterns are now referred to internationally as Lotto, Crivelli, Bellini after the most famous artists who included them in their paintings. But Holbein was not the first or the only artist to paint the type of Ushak now associated with him. The geometric motif repeated in the field of Turkmen and Turkish rugs is called *gul* (rose), and one pattern variation is now known as a 'Memling gul' after Memling the artist. Nineteenth-century Western interiors in paintings show a different type of 'Turkey Carpet', still predominantly red with blue and green tracery, but coarse and heavy. Soon this was imitated and mass-produced by machines.

45

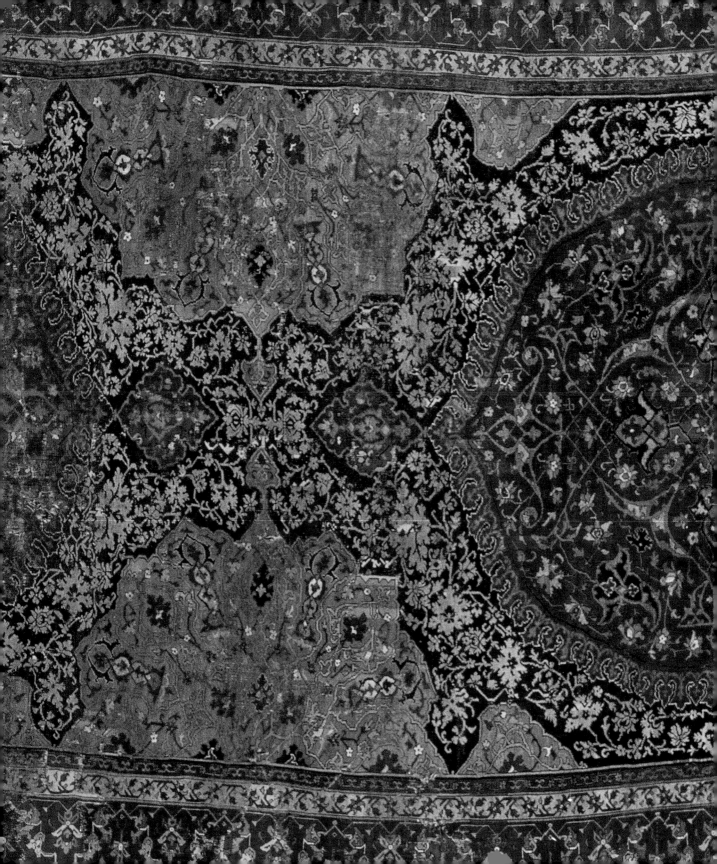

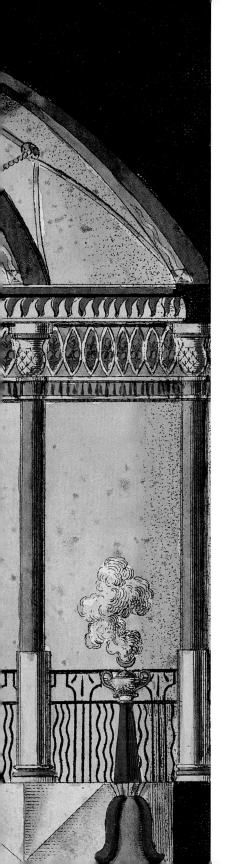

TENTS AND PAVILIONS

The ancestors of the Ottomans were nomadic Turkish tribes who migrated with their flocks and fierce outriders from the Steppes of Central Asia to Anatolia, where they eventually settled. Home was the circular felt tent, the *yurt,* comfortably and methodically organized inside, practical and easily transportable. The relationship between tents and Ottoman architecture is extremely close. Within the tent, tightly woven bands reinforced with leather replaced certain architectural load-bearing members, and embroidery and appliqué not only provided colour and decoration, but also strengthened and insulated the walls. On ascending the throne, each Sultan ordered an accession tent, a magnificent embroidered construction of silk, with silver and gold threads. The Sultan's palace in Constantinople, Topkapi Sarayi (the Palace of the Cannon Gate), is a huge tent complex built in stone. Whether on campaign or not, the Ottoman army spent at least five months under canvas, and to achieve this every aspect of the camp was strictly regimented. Those whose job it was to pitch the tents went ahead of the Sultan and his retinue. The camp was laid out in a logical, functional design, which can clearly be seen in Turkish miniatures. It was said that the Ottomans 'lodge more grandly in the field than at home'. The cat's cradle of guy-ropes made it extremely difficult to penetrate the camp at night, and mutiny was declared when the ropes of the commanders' tents were cut.

At the Siege of Vienna in 1683, the Ottomans erected a canvas city beside the Austrian capital, but bigger, and much better ordered than Vienna itself. The Austrians, who had been brought up to tremble at stories of these bloodthirsty infidels, wondered at the sight of soldiers who even planted gardens in front of their embroidered dwellings. After the battle, when Sobieski III of Poland entered the camp, he wrote of the Ottoman General, the Grand Vizier Kara Mustafa Pasha: '...and what delicacies the Vizier had in his tents it is hard to describe. He had a bath, a garden and fountains, rabbits and cats, even a parrot, but this was flying, and we could not catch it....'

Europe marvelled at the treasures left behind and, indeed, at the Ottoman tented city itself, which was captured and distributed after the Siege of Vienna.

Ottoman tents were erected in the grounds of palaces and stately homes, and, as the original fabric decayed, imitation tents of stone and brick were built as follies. Eighteenth-century Europe fell in love with the Turkish tents: a Turkish Tent was erected at Vauxhall Gardens in 1744, and in the landscaped gardens of Painshill, Surrey, the Turkish tent, now cast in limewashed brick and cement, has been recently restored. The Empress Josephine demanded a Tent Room at Malmaison, and in Maria Edgeworth's novel, *The Absentee* (1812), Mr Soho, the 'first architectural upholsterer of the age', tempts Lady Clonbrony, arrived in London from Ireland, with Turkish tent drapery, seraglio ottomans, and 'Trebisond trellice paper.' In the last summer of his life, King George IV of England dined frequently in the Turkish tents erected on the shore of Virginia Water, and everywhere pavilions and kiosks, even European and American bandstands, such as that in New York's Central Park, follow the design of the Ottoman tent.

But although the layouts of encampments were organized to the very last detail, Ottoman gardens were, until the eighteenth century, much more informal affairs, with perfumed pathways meandering through flowers and shrubs, shaded by trees, and cooled by waterways and fountains.

Sultan Ahmet III's Ambassador to Paris, Mehmet Said Effendi, who arrived in France in 1720, was very impressed by the gardens of Louis XV.

53

The Sultan's most beloved palace, Sa'adabad, or Eternal Happiness, was influenced by prints of Versailles (still in the Topkapi library), and the plans of the château of Marly, sent by the Ambassador from Paris. It was built in the meadows known as the Sweet Waters of Asia, beside two streams leading into the Golden Horn. The garden was planted in the Versailles manner, with straight rows of trees and square flowerbeds, but the palace and kiosks were still very Turkish, with wide projecting eaves, golden domes and walls painted in bright colours.

PAGE 54: Ceiling of the Twin Pavilions, or Heir's Apartments, in the Topkapi Sarayi, Istanbul. A radiating sunburst represents the heavens' dome.
PAGE 55: Interior of Sa'adullah Pasha *yali*, Istanbul. The domed ceiling, painted with rope-like beading, gives the feeling of a tent roof.
OPPOSITE: Ottoman Art Nouveau Pavilion, Beylerbey Palace, 1861–64, designed by the Balyan brothers. The Art Nouveau movement borrowed heavily from Oriental sources.
ABOVE: Colour plate from J. B. Papworth, 'Garden Seats' from *Rural Residences*, London, 1818. Europe marvelled at the Ottoman tented city, captured and distributed after the Siege of Vienna in 1683. Ottoman tents were erected in the grounds of palaces and stately homes, then imitations were built as follies, as 18th-century Europe fell in love with Turkish tents.

OPPOSITE: *A Corner of the Harem Garden*, by Alberto Pasini, 1877. Pasini spent from 1867 to 1869 in Constantinople. In a letter to a friend he described seeing groups of women forming the most unexpected harmonies of colours, and this made him think of living and talking flowers, against a background of the azure waters of the Bosphorus, with its banks flanked with gems of painted villas.

LEFT: Gilded bower, also known as the Iftar Kiosk, built by Sultan Ibrahim on the terrace of the Fourth Court of the Tokapi Sarayi, overlooking the Golden Horn and the old city of Istanbul.

BELOW: One of two wooden porches, like kiosks in design, of the Zeki Pasha *yali,* built on the Bosphorus, 1895.

SWEET WATERS

'Sweet Waters of Asia' is the name of a once-beautiful meadow on the Golden Horn where two streams flow together, a favourite picnic place for the ladies, including those of the Imperial Harem. Often they went there by boat, from the sides of which hung little gilded fish suspended on chains, or trailing silks embroidered with fishes. Lord Byron wrote:

EACH VILLA ON THE BOSPHORUS LOOKS AT A SCREEN,
NEW PAINTED, OR A PRETTY OPERA-SCENE.

He was thinking of the grand wooden houses on the waterfront serving as summer retreats. Until the eighteenth century, the shores of the Bosphorus were the densely wooded hunting preserve of the Sultans, and only a few high-ranking officials were allowed to build there. Gradually vineyards, gardens and orchards appeared, different villages specializing in different fruits: Ortakoy in cherries, Meçidiyekoy in

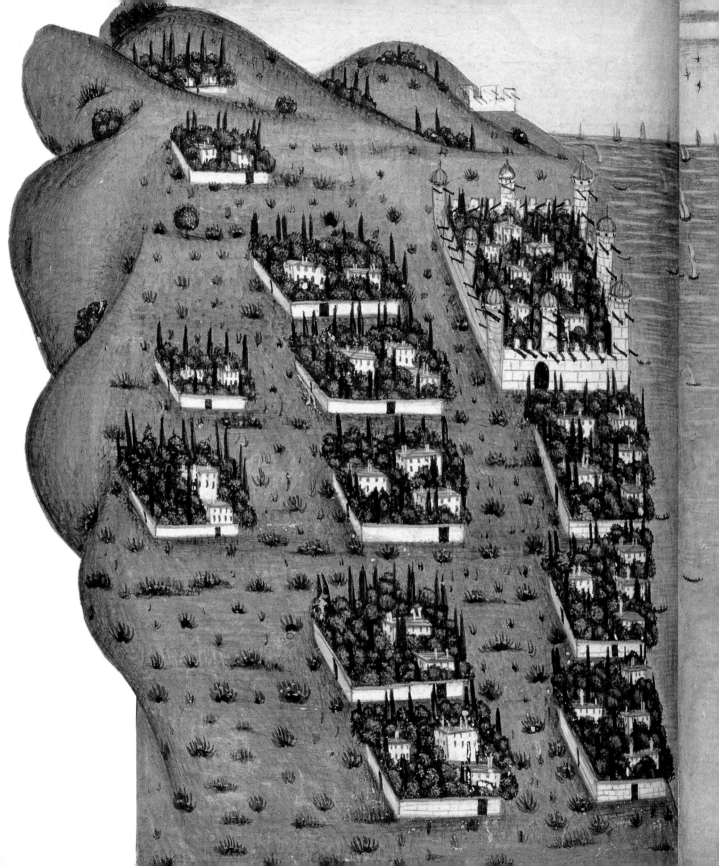

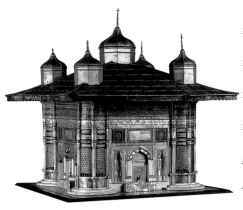

mulberries. In the eighteenth century Ahmet III built new palaces along the shores, and made gifts of land to favourite courtiers. Beautiful wooden villas, called *yalis*, from the Greek *yialos*, seashore, began to appear against the green backdrop of forested hillsides. The dominant colour was 'Ottoman rose'– Sa'adullah Pasha *yali* is still painted in this shade. Gardens behind these summer residences contained pools, winding canals, marble cascades, and were shaded by trees and shrubs.

As in Venice, the main façade of the waterside houses gives on to the water, and, as there is no tide, rooms were built on the same level as the Bosphorus for those inside to enjoy the sight and sound of water

PAGE 60: Sa'adullah Pasha *yali*, painted in 'Ottoman rose', 1760s.
PAGE 61: Kibrish *yali*, 1775.
PAGES 62–63: Houses on the Bosphorus, Turkish manuscript, 1738–39, British Library, London.
ABOVE: 1907 model of a fountain erected by Ahmet III in 1729; Topkapi Sarayi Museum.

and the play of reflected light on the tiles. Many *yalis* were built with their cantilevered bay windows actually jutting out over the water. Some rooms had channels of water cut in the floor, and in others jets of cooling water cascaded musically from floor or wall fountains. Wherever the Ottomans chose to build, there were fountains. After Mehmet's conquest of Constantinople, every neighbourhood was given a fountain, largely funded by individuals as a mark of piety. Muslims always wash before prayers, and every mosque provides water for this. Fountains drew either from the main water system or from individual springs. Eighteenth-century fountains were often free-standing, like ornate little pavilions, and also sold fruit juices and sherbets.

The surfaces of water, marble and glazed ceramic created an ambiance of cool tranquillity. The gardens outside were echoed on painted surfaces and tiles, predominantly in green, blue and turquoise. PAGES 66-67: CLOCKWISE FROM CENTRE ABOVE: Fountain, Arab Hall, Leighton House, London. Then, all located in the Topkapi Sarayi, Istanbul: Fountain of Suleyman the Magnificent, Chamber of Petitions; fountain in the Fourth Court (an original feature of the palace, remodelled during the 17th century); three-tiered fountain in Murad III's bedroom; Vestibule of the Fountain, Harem.

TURKISH INTERIORS

Turkey is a land of earthquakes, and Istanbul stands on a fault line. Apart from the great stone mosques and the Sultan's palace, Topkapi Sarayi, many of the buildings, and most of the domestic dwellings, used to be constructed of wood, which causes less damage in an earthquake. But wood is very vulnerable to fire, and the city has been devastated by flames many times. In 1574 a fire started in the kitchens of the Topkapi Sarayi and reduced these and surrounding buildings to ruins. In 1757 a fire that began on the Golden Horn spread in ten directions and destroyed half the city within its walls. Despite building innovations in the late nineteenth century, the inhabitants were destined to live with the threat of fire for a long time. Le Corbusier witnessed a city fire in 1911 – 'this wild dragon lashing around'.

The traditional Ottoman house is eminently practical. Until the nineteenth century and the introduction of reforms intended to bring Turkey closer to her European neighbours, very little furniture was used. Space was segregated, as was daily life. Beds were simply mattresses, aired with the rest of the bedding in the morning, then rolled and stored until night time. Meals were served on a large tray, set on little folding legs, all cleared away after eating. A large brazier, *mangal,* substituted for a fireplace. Low seating, *sedir,* was built in on three sides of a room, and covered with fabrics, kilims and cushions. Rugs on the floor did not suffer from undue wear and tear as they do in the West, because outdoor shoes were discarded before entering, and replaced by soft indoor slippers.

PAGE 69: Kibrish *yali*, 18th century. The Winter Garden with its marble fountain and intricate pebble floor, is decorated in a style inherited from ancient Byzantium.
PAGE 70: Wall recesses clad in Iznik tiles, and a door of the *harem* apartments inlaid with mother-of-pearl and tortoiseshell; in the Topkapi Sarayi, Istanbul.
PAGE 71: The Fruit Room of Ahmet III, painted during the Tulip Reign (1703–30); Topkapi Sarayi, Istanbul.
ABOVE: Cupboard with doors inlaid with fruitwood and mother-of-pearl; private collection, Paris. Furniture like this was made from the mid-19th century, influenced by Mahmud II's reforms, as European notions of interior decoration arrived.

The basic shape of the traditional house is cruciform, with a main central room, often domed, and rooms leading from this in four directions. The principal room, a large reception room on an upper floor, is called the *sofa*. This can also describe a low raised bay, usually covered with carpets. On the ground floor there might be pebble mosaics, especially in the *yalis,* an inheritance from the Byzantine city. Painted ceilings, *trompe l'oeil* and murals are common, and ceilings, windows, frames and walls are carved and decorated with coloured and gilded flower motifs, rosettes and arabesques. Wall niches display pots of flowers or glass incense burners.

In the nineteenth century, as wealthy Ottomans abandoned the traditional built-in sitting areas in favour of European settees and chairs, a new style emerged, combining Western ideas with an Eastern flavour. One of the more successful pieces of furniture was a round and multi-sided occasional table, inlaid with mother-of-pearl. Carved, tasselled and inlaid furniture was avidly sought to furnish 'Orientalist' interiors and harmonize with Orientalist paintings, and these were often displayed on mother-of-pearl inlaid easels. Western homes featured the new 'divan' associated with life *à l'orientale,* inviting lounging and relaxation, and the Turkish bath, *hamam*, with its decorative tiles became the very height of fashion.

The earliest tiles made in Iznik (ancient Nicaea) used a palette of blues, sage green and manganese purple. This changed radically after 1551, and for a period in the second half of the sixteenth century a rich raised coral predominated. Known as 'Armenian bole', the red was

mixed from a clay previously used by apothecaries for medicinal purposes. In the next century this 'sealing-wax' colour began to lose its quality. The acquisition of a brilliantly coloured Islamic tile prompted French ceramicist Joseph-Théodore Deck to explore and revive Middle Eastern ceramic techniques in the creation, from the mid-nineteenth century, of his own unique art. Deck was the first of the artist-potters in what became a widespread revolution in European ceramics, keenly studying the shapes and colours of Islamic ceramics, and becoming especially interested in those of Iznik, which he sometimes copied directly. At the same time, other ceramicists, William de Morgan, for example, were also looking East for inspiration.

Louis Tiffany's influence on taste in late nineteenth-century New York was as powerful as Arthur Liberty's in London, and his delight in Islamic art was more pronounced. The roots of the Art Nouveau movement that Tiffany and Liberty's did so much to nurture, lay in the arabesques and calligraphy of Islam, and the sinuous plant forms of Oriental art. Istanbul is a veritable treasure chest of glorious Art Nouveau architecture and interiors, comparable to Paris, Vienna or Brussels, yet this seems to be a well kept secret.

BELOW LEFT: A narrow side table inlaid with mother-of-pearl, possibly 18th century; private collection.

ABOVE: Detail of inlaid mother-of-pearl door in the Topkapi Sarayi, incorporating a favourite Ottoman motif – the *çintamani,* triple dots in a triangular layout. Originally a Buddhist symbol this became the blazon of the Timurid Dynasty (that of Timur, 'Tamburlain', and his descendants in the 14th and 15th centuries). Combined with undulating lines, it suggests leopard and tiger pelts with their own royal and heroic significance.

PAGES 74–75 FROM LEFT: Walls stencilled with carnations, copied from an Ottoman velvet, hallway; author's house, London. The carved wooden *musrabiye* screen looking down on the Fountain Room; Leighton House, London. Frederick, Lord Leighton, the Orientalist painter, visited Constantinople in 1867, and the most notable result of his travels in the Ottoman world was the Arab Hall, designed by George Aitchison and 1877–79 added to Leighton's Holland Park home. Pierre Loti wrote *Aziyadé* (1879) and other novels about love in faraway lands. He transformed his family home (now Musée Pierre Loti, Rochefort) with a mosque and Eastern rooms, the room that had been his Great-Aunt Berthe's becoming the Turkish Salon.

73

RIGHT: Set for a picnic, a raised wooden platform for entertaining, outside the restored *konak* (villa), and studio of artist Sema Menteseoglu. It is situated in the countryside of southern Turkey, near Dalaman. The traditional Ottoman house did not have separate rooms for sleeping or dining, and food was carried and served on large trays which were set on little collapsible legs.

OPPOSITE: Artist Sema Menteseoglu has lovingly restored the house built in 1878 by her great-grandfather, Ali Riza Pasha, in the grounds of his forebears' ruined palace. The hall serves as a study.

76

HAREM
AND HAMAM

Harem means that which is forbidden, protected or sacred. The women's quarters were the *haremlik*, the men's, the *selamlik*. Only the master of the household had right of access to the *haremlik*. *Oda* means chamber; an odalisque, therefore, is a woman of the chamber.

The female hierarchy of the Sultan's *harem* was complicated; every woman occupied a position according to her age, status, and the point at which she arrived in her harem education. Ruled by the Sultan's mother, it had its own personnel, methods of administration and customs. Positions of responsibility were held by women who had advanced in every part of the harem training, but who had been passed by as far as the chance to become a favourite, *kadin*, was concerned. Alternatively, they might be married off to high-ranking officials. A palace-trained wife was an asset to an ambitious man.

The young women were taught basic skills, as well as singing, dancing and the all-important embroidery. Each received *pashmaklik*, literally 'slipper money', for her own use, and 'bundlewomen' brought jewels, fabrics, ribbons and other luxuries for them to buy. The higher the status, the more opportunity women had to invest their money and

do good works, and a number of mosques, hospitals and schools were paid for by the sisters, favourites, wives and mothers of sultans.

The Western notion of a debauched Sultan with a taste for obese women is based on Sultan Ibrahim, who succeeded in 1640. One of mad Ibrahim's particular sexual fancies was fulfilled by 'Sugar Lump', a vast Armenian discovered after a nationwide search. Some Sultans, however, even with the availability of a *harem*, preferred a monogamous relationship. Suleyman the Magnificent was so much in love with Roxelana that he scandalized the Imperial court by marrying her.

An important ritual in every woman's life was the weekly visit to the *hamam,* the baths. 'It is the women's coffee-house, where all news of the town is told, scandal invented, et cetera.' So wrote Lady Mary Wortley Montagu, describing her first visit to a Turkish bath in Sofia, while travelling with her husband's embassy to Turkey in 1716.

PAGE 78: *The Reception,* John Frederick Lewis, 1873; Yale Center for British Art, Paul Mellon collection. Thackeray described Lewis as a 'Turkified European', a 'languid Lotus-eater'.
PAGE 79: Turkish *hamam* pattens, wood and silver gilt, worn to keep the feet dry.
PAGES 80–81: The Reception Room in the Harem apartments, Topkapi Sarayi, Istanbul. The walls are painted and set with Iznik tiles, and the shutters are inlaid with mother-of-pearl.
OPPOSITE: *L'Esclave Blanche* (The White Slave), Le Comte du Nouy, 1888; Musée des Beaux Arts, Nantes. A pale-skinned Circassian is seated on velvet cushions, *yastik,* and draped in an embroidered Turkish towel.
ABOVE: J. E. Debat-Ponsan, *Le Massage,* 1883; Musée des Augustins, Toulouse, showing Iznik tiles in an authentic setting.

ABOVE: *The Odalisque and the Slave*, Jean-Auguste Dominique Ingres, 1839; Fogg Art Museum, Cambridge, Mass. Ingres was inspired by a passage in Lady Mary Wortley Montagu's *Turkish Embassy Letters* describing her first visit to a Turkish bath in Sofia. Ingres copied the passage into his sketchbook, and throughout his life returned time and again to the subject of his imaginings. This is a particularly fanciful scene.

A hundred years later, in 1817, the young Ingres copied a French translation of Lady Mary's description into his sketchbook. It contained the key passage: 'I believe on the whole there were two hundred women…the first sofas were covered with cushions and rich carpets, on which sat ladies, and on the second their slaves behind them, but without distinction of rank and dress, all being in the state of nature…so many fine women were naked in different postures, some working, others drinking coffee or sherbet, and many negligently lying on their cushions while their slaves…were employed in braiding their hair….' Ingres's many subsequent studies of naked odalisques and scenes set in imaginary Turkish baths culminated forty-five years later in *Le Bain Turc* (1863).

Of her conversations with the Pasha, Ahmet Bey, in whose house in Sofia Lord and Lady Wortley Montagu stayed en route to Turkey, she wrote: 'I have frequent disputes with him concerning the differences of our customs, particularly the confinements of women. He assures me there is nothing at all in it; only, he says we have the advantage that when our wives cheat us, nobody knows it.' These discussions might well have been the source of one of Lady Mary's favourite themes, that the supposed subjugation of women in the Islamic world in fact gave them power. When Lady Mary and her husband arrived in the capital, one of the first things she did was to seek out Turkish women, and she later learnt Turkish so that she could converse with them more freely.

BELOW: *Turkish Sultana*, Lucknow, 1810–20, a Mughal interpretation of a Western Orientalist painting; Chester Beatty Library, Dublin. Mughal ruling families, who had Turkish antecedents, often took Ottoman wives. OVERLEAF CLOCKWISE FROM LEFT: *Hamam* scenes: from a manuscript of Nizami's poetry, 16th century, Chester Beatty Library, Dublin; miniature, 17th century, Topkapi Sarayi Museum; from an erotic poem by Fezil Bey, Turkish, 18th century, British Library, London. Lady with hennaed toes and fingers washing herself, by Abdullah Buhari, 1741–42, Topkapi Sarayi Museum.

85

IN TURKISH GUISE

In 1510, at the court of Henry VIII, the Earl of Essex and his entourage appeared at the Shrove Sunday banquet 'appareled after Turkey fasshion, in long robes of Bawdkin [an Oriental silk], powdered with gold, hattes on their headdes of Crimosyn Velvet, with great rolles of gold, girded with two swordes called Cimeteries [scimitars].'

In Constantinople, Western merchants often wore Ottoman dress and grew their beards Muslim fashion, and it was said that, although the Dutch and English could pass as Turks, the French could not. European ambassadors and other travellers of means often included an artist in their retinue, and there was a growing market in Europe for paintings, prints and illustrated books depicting the costumes and the wonders of the East. One of the first of these artists, Jean-Baptiste Vanmour (1671–1737), who arrived in Constantinople with the French Ambassador de Ferriol, certainly contributed to the fashion for Europeans to be painted in Oriental clothes. Members of the Ottoman court, even the Sultan himself, allowed themselves to be painted by Vanmour, and his book of engravings of Ottoman costumes, first published in 1712–13, was reprinted time and again to meet popular demand in Europe.

The portrayal of the Turk in masques, ballets opera and drama was merely a foil for European

heroism, or worse, an object of derision. Most hero ic tales at the end of the sixteenth century featured shipwrecks, pirates, star-crossed lovers and murderous Turks. The renegade of drama, an Englishman who had 'turned Turk', was as much an English invention as 'the Moor', representing all that was Oriental and alien to England. The first dramatic representation of the Christian convert to Islam appears in Thomas Kyd's *The Tragedye of Solyman and Perseda*' in 1588, followed by Thomas Heywood's *The Fair Maid of the West* (1604–10), then John Mason's *The Turk* (1607).

After the Siege of Vienna in 1683, theatres were filled with plays and operas in which the efforts of wicked (and polygamous) Turks to despoil virtuous Western heroines, usually princesses, were foiled by gallant Western heroes. These were true precursors of the 'rescue opera' genre. When Mozart's *Die Entführung aus dem Serail* (Escape from the Seraglio) was first performed in 1782, a century had gone by since the Siege of Vienna, and the passion for Turkish themes was at its height. Several centuries later, the opera is regularly performed in Turkish in Istanbul, inside the Topkapi Sarayi itself.

From the time of the military clashes in the fifteenth century, the Ottoman Empire strongly influenced the musical tradition of the West. The Turkish troops were led by a military band composed of

PAGE 88: *The Sultana,* Charles Van Loo, 18th century; Musée Cheret, Nice. In 1772, Van Loo was commissioned to produce cartoons for a series of Gobelins tapestries, showing the customs of the Levant. They were to include five episodes of a Sultana's typical day. PAGE 89 ABOVE: *Lady Mary Wortley Montagu and Her Son,* by Baptiste Vanmour, National Portrait Gallery, London. PAGE 89 BELOW: Perfume holder, Dresden, 18th century, enamelled and jewelled silver and gold; Museo degli Argenti, Florence. This is an example of *turqueries* – items made in the West, particularly in the 18th century – that evoked the mysterious East. ABOVE: Turkish quadriglia, from a ceremonial procession at the court of Louis XIV in 1662.

trumpets, fifes, drums and cymbals. The idea soon caught on in Europe, and even the janissaries' *chaghana*, a crescent-shaped standard hung with horse tails and bells, carried before the regiment, became a favourite in the West, its name, in English, transliterated into Jingling Johnny.

As part of his modernization plans, Mahmud II abolished the Janissaries in 1826, and decided his army should march to a Western-style band. In due course, Giuseppe Donizetti, brother of the composer Gaetano Donizetti, was given command of the Imperial Band and later the Imperial Ottoman School of Music. In later years, he trained and conducted an orchestra of harem ladies for the entertainment of Abdulhamid, the opera-loving Sultan who insisted that the tragic endings should be rewritten – in his own versions, Violetta was restored to health and lived happily ever after; Mimi's little hand was no longer frozen and she, too, revived; and *Rigoletto*, the Sultan's favourite opera, was retitled *L'Opéra de la Fille du Roi*.

ABOVE: '*Turqueries*' style, a French painting on glass, showing an imaginary scene *à la Turque,* 18th century; private collection. BELOW: Group in Turkish costume, detail from an engraving by Cochin, of a masked ball held by Louis XV at Versailles to celebrate the marriage of the Dauphin; 18th century; Louvre, Paris.

91

After the Treaty of Karlowitz in 1699, Turco-European relations relaxed, and with the arrival of Mehmet Efendi, the first Ottoman ambassador to the French court, in 1720, the fashion for all things Turkish and exotic rapidly spread. 'Turcomania' reached a new pitch when the young Sa'aid Efendi, son of Mehmet, arrived in Paris in 1742 as the new Ambassador. The King's mistress, Madame de Pompadour, posed as a Sultana for three paintings by Charles

ABOVE: A child's *entari*, or overgarment, 18th century, cotton embroidered with silk and gold thread.
BELOW: A child's trousers with integral leather bootees, 17th century. Both are in the Topkapi Sarayi Museum, Istanbul.
OPPOSITE: J. E. Liotard, *Turkish Woman and her Slave*, 1742; Musée d'Art et d'Histoire, Geneva. They wear pattens to keep their feet dry in the *hamam*, and the woman's fingers are hennaed. The Swiss artist was known as 'The Turk', not only for his portraits of Europeans in Ottoman dress, but also because he grew his beard and dressed like a Turk.

Van Loo. Not to be upstaged, her successor, Madame du Barry, also commissioned Van Loo to paint four portraits of her *en sultane*. It was rumoured that these were to rekindle Louis XV's ardour with the suggestion of Oriental promise.

Ladies wore Circassian robes, and rouged their cheeks with 'Circassian bloom'. By 1778 turbans were the rage; by 1781, little Turkish caps with feathers. Jane Austen wore a 'Mamluk' cap with a crescent-shaped ornament for holding a feather. Turkish tales were written with more authenticity, and Lady Mary Wortley Montagu's *Turkish Embassy Letters* (1763), describing her stay in Constantinople in 1716, was an instant success, as was an earlier book by Giovanni Marana, an Italian living in France in the seventeenth century. Marana wrote in the character of a Turk visiting Paris, and these fictional letters to his friends, *Letters Writ by a Turkish Spy,* were very popular throughout the eighteenth century.

In the nineteenth century, Hans Christian Andersen was one of the many travellers who visited Turkey, and his sketchbooks and letters home are full of drawings of dervishes, the Muslim ascetics. In his story *The Flying Trunk,* the hero is a merchant's son, a poor boy who owns nothing but a dressing gown and slippers. Magic delivers him into the land of the Turks, where he feels totally at ease because 'all the Turks wear dressing gowns and slippers'. All the characters in the British pantomime *Aladdin* do so still.

LEFT: *Victoria, Princess Royal in Turkish Costume*, by Sir W. C. Ross, 1850; The Royal Collection, HM Queen Elizabeth II. This miniature of the ten-year-old princess (later through marriage Empress of Germany, and mother to Emperor William II), was given to Queen Victoria by Prince Albert for her birthday in May 1850.

ABOVE: Costume designs for Turks in the opera *La Pellegrina,* 1589; Biblioteca Nazionale, Florence.

OPPOSITE: *The Countess Mary of Coventry,* J. E. Liotard, *c.* 1750. Musée d'Art et d'Histoire, Geneva. Liotard's portrait of the Countess shows her with an embroidered *entari* (overgarment) and silk *shalwar* (harem pants)*,* and at her feet a medallion Ushak carpet. The same carpet appears in other portraits, which seems to suggest that Liotard owned it and used it as a studio prop.

COFFEE AND TOBACCO

Coffee, a native of Ethiopia, was first cultivated in the Yemen, where it was used in Sufi ceremonies. The name derives from *kahveh,* originally a poetic name for wine. Syria and the Yemen had been part of the Ottoman empire since the early sixteenth century, and the first public coffee house in Constantinople was opened by two Syrians in 1554. Three years later they returned home with a small fortune.

It seems as if tobacco, introduced from America to Constantinople by English merchants in 1601, was destined to be coffee's natural accompaniment. At first it was denounced in mosques, and in 1633 Murad IV forbade smoking on pain of death. Finally, in 1647 the Mufti of Constantinople allowed tobacco. By the end of the eighteenth century it was not only one of the main exports of the Ottoman Empire, but also one of the principal means to convey status, indicated by the length, beauty and material of a pipe and its mouthpiece. The long stem might be cherry or jasmine wood, mouthpieces might be of amber, ivory or hippopotamus tooth, and pale lemon amber was considered particularly fine. The *nargileh,* or water pipe, was available in coffee houses and clients brought their own mouthpiece to smoke tobacco and opium through soothing rose-scented water.

PAGE 96: Turkish coffee house, detail of a 16th-century miniature; Chester Beatty Library, Dublin PAGE 97 ABOVE: Ming dynasty porcelain cups, encrusted with gold and jewels in Turkey in the 17th century; Topkapi Sarayi Museum, Istanbul. PAGE 97 BELOW, AND OPPOSITE: Serving coffee, engravings by Martin Engelbrecht, Augsburg *c.* 1735; Bibliothèque des Arts Decoratifs, Paris. ABOVE FROM LEFT: Second, Turkish flask for water or wine; then a ewer of *tombak*, gilt-copper; next is a censor for burning perfumes and incense, then the traditional Oriental coffee pot adopted in the West for coffee and chocolate; third from right, dishes for serving *sherbet,* sorbet; far right, coffee pot in the Iznik style, made by the Florentine factory of Cantagalli, after 1870, whose French inscription is from a Turkish recipe for coffee: 'Black as the devil/Hot as hell/Pure as an angel/Sweet as love).' BELOW LEFT: Street coffee vendor in Constantinople, 17th-century Dutch engraving.

By 1700 coffee and tobacco were firmly established throughout Europe. Coffee houses in Marseilles and Venice fostered the habit, and, soon after 1650, one opened in St Michael's Alley, Cornhill, London. The Turk's Head became the most popular name for coffee houses, which adopted as their symbol a turbanned Moor, a 'Sultan's head', or a coffee pot. The first handbill against coffee appeared in 1652 – the habit was thought to encourage Englishmen in apostasy to Islam. In France the following year, attempts were also made to discredit the drink, this time by the wine merchants. *The Women's Petition Against Coffee,* published in London in 1674, complained that men were never at home but were always in coffee houses, and that, furthermore, the drink rendered them incapable of fulfilling their conjugal duties. Coffee has been blamed for ailments ranging from impotence, weight loss, melancholia, to hysteria, and alternatively praised as a cure for ailments ranging from leprosy to – impotence.

Vienna's fame as a coffee capital dates from the Ottoman Siege of Vienna in 1683, when the retreating Turkish armies left behind sacks of green coffee beans. An interpreter, Franz George Kischitsky,

prepared the beans in the Ottoman fashion, and sold cups of coffee from door to door. It is said that the croissant (crescent) was a celebratory cake from this time – this could be true, as layered pastries are thought to be a legacy from the Steppes.

In 1669 Mehmet IV sent his emissary Suleyman Aga to the court of Louis XIV. A palace was put at his disposal and rumours quickly spread that this had been filled with Ottoman delights. Visitors were offered coffee, but unsweetened (the Turks at that time preferred it flavoured with ambergris). French ladies surreptitiously sweetened it with sugar they brought 'for the ambassadors's birds'. Sweetmeats were also served, rosewater was sprinkled on the guests' hands from a narrow-necked bottle and rooms were scented with burning perfumes. The King was so intrigued by the Ottoman envoy that he asked Molière to include a Turkish episode in his new play *Le Bourgeois Gentilhomme*, first performed on 14 October 1670.

Porcelain factories and silversmiths filled the demand for the tiny coffee cups and long-spouted ewer-shaped pots based on those of the East. Turkish cups had no handles, so enterprising jewellers developed containers for these – Switzerland in particular specialized in making gem-studded and enamelled *zarf*s for the Ottoman Empire.

LEFT: *The Sultana*, by Charles Van Loo, mid-18th century; Musée des Arts Decoratifs, Paris. Turcophilia reached a peak in Europe in the 18th century, when all things Oriental, but particularly Turkish, were especially modish. Here Madame de Pompadour, the mistress of King Louis XV of France, is dressed in Turkish costume, and is being served coffee by a black servant. La Pompadour posed as a Sultana for three paintings by Charles Van Loo. Not to be outshone, Madame du Barry, her successor, commissioned four similar paintings of herself from the same artist.

ABOVE: *Moscow Coffee Party*, Giuseppe Tominz mid-19th century ; Narodna Galeria, Ljubljana. By this time, drinking coffee with something sweet to eat was no longer an exquisite pastime with Oriental overtones, but an everyday bourgeois pleasure, especially in Central and Eastern Europe.

ABOVE: *Self-portrait*, by Horace
Vernet, (1789–1863); Hermitage
Museum, St Petersburg.

RIGHT: *Slave Market, Constantinople,*
by Sir William Allen, 1838; National
Gallery of Scotland, Edinburgh.
Vernet strikes a languid pose with
a long Turkish *chubuk*, and in the
foreground of Allan's picture, smokers
have the option of pipe or *nargileh*,
the water pipe nicknamed the 'hubble-
bubble'. The costumes are accurate,
except that, by the time Allen's
painting was completed, officials had
exchanged their turbans for the fez.
Allan, like his friend Sir Walter Scott,
believed in fictionalizing facts.
Conditions of slavery in the Ottoman
Empire usually compared favourably
with those of servants in Europe.
It was customary to free slaves after
a maximum of nine years' service,
but it was common for slaves to refuse
manumission, in which case the master
and his heirs were legally bound to
maintain them for life. Within fifteen
years of Allan's imaginary scene, the
slave market in Istanbul was closed,
though slavery continued.

OPPOSITE: *Capitals and pilasters from the Temple of Apollo, Didyma*, watercolour by William Pars, 1765; British Museum, London.

ABOVE: Gold snuff box with an inscription in small diamonds. 1838; private collection.

LEFT ABOVE: *Sir Thomas Phillips in Eastern Costume*, watercolour by Richard Dadd; private collection. Dadd travelled to the Middle East in 1842 as artist/companion to Phillips, a wealthy barrister. On Dadd's return, suffering delusions, he killed his father, and in 1843 was committed to Broadmoor where he spent the rest of his life, and where he produced Orientalist scenes as well as his famous fairy paintings. Ottoman poets wrote of 'the four cushions of pleasure' – tobacco, coffee, opium and wine – and this portrait suggests something more potent than tobacco.

LEFT BELOW: Photograph of the French writer Pierre Loti (1850–1923) smoking in Turkey, with his dragoman (interpreter), Choukri.

ORIENT EXPRESS

CHEMINS DE FER PARIS-LYON-MÉDITERRANÉE
SIMPLON-ORIENT-EXPRESS

LONDRES-PARIS-BUCAREST-ATHÈNES-CONSTANTINOPLE

Racehorses all claim descent from the fleet Turkish and Arab breeds whose stamina carried the Ottomans west. Centuries later, with the advent of the railway's 'iron horse', modern travel and tourism arrived at the portals of the Ottoman Empire. On 12 August 1888 the Orient Express steamed into Sirkeçi Station. In due course, further tracks were laid to build the Constantinople-to-Baghdad line. To accommodate the travellers, the Compagnie de Wagons-Lits built Pera Palas Hotel on the heights above Galata, conveniently placed for all the foreign embassies. Agatha Christie, author of *Murder on the Orient Express*, whose archaeologist husband worked in the Middle East, was a regular traveller. To build the railway, Ottoman kiosks and much of the Byzantine sea wall were destroyed, and also an ancient grove in the palace gardens. Every Wednesday night, the Lord of the Djinns had held council there, and locals lamented; 'Where will he go now?' Even the Lord of the Djinns had to bow to progress.

The reforming Mahmud II, who reigned 1808–39, was determined to ensure a strong Ottoman presence in Europe, building new palaces and neoclassical barracks to make Constantinople, like Vienna and St Petersburg, an imperial power statement, In 1815, he moved from the Topkapi Sarayi to Dolmahbaçe. Gradually the old palace became the haunt of ghosts, discarded harem women, and the eunuchs and slaves who cared for them. The Sultan's envoy in London informed him that the European press was critical of the Turkish practice of building in wood, so vulnerable to fire.

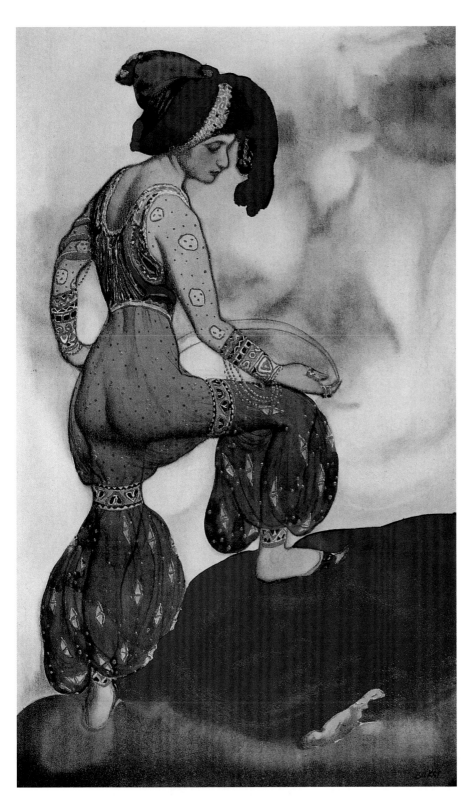

OPPOSITE: Poster for the Orient Express by Roger Broders, 1921. **LEFT** 'The Blue Sultana', design for *Schéhérezade*, Ballets Russes, by Léon Bakst, 1911; private collection. It was to Turkish Central Asia that Bakst and Sergei Diaghilev turned for the vivid silks that amazed the world when their Ballets Russes arrived in Paris in 1909. And it was partly the Turkish tones in the music of such Russian composers as Borodin, Glinka and Rimsky-Korsakov that entranced Western ears. In Paris, Paul Poiret designed harem pants and turbans, and opened an interior design company to provide the appropriate setting for them, in which women smoked perfumed Turkish cigarettes in long holders and wore scents whose names evoked Eastern exoticism.

The Sultan decided to send young Turks to study architecture and engineering in Europe, and to bring European architects to Turkey. In their wake, Art Nouveau returned to its Eastern roots. Modernization of the army, initiated by Selim III (who reigned 1789–1807), was continued under Mahmud along Prussian lines. Mahmud's palaces were furnished with Sèvres porcelain and fashionable French furniture, he dined in the Western manner and drank champagne every night, and coffee was served with saucers, sugar, even sugar tongs. Glass factories produced European/Turkish style wares, including Beykoz which resembled Bohemian glass, and *'çesme bulbul'* (nightingale's eye), with fine ribbon-like spirals of opaque blue

or white, imitating a sixteenth-century Venetian pattern. By 1900, Europeanized ceramics and gilt wood upholstered furniture, called by decorators today 'Louis Farouk', became a fashion that soon spread to other parts of the Empire and beyond. French began to replace Persian as the second language of the court, and newsboys offered papers in a dozen languages. The more conservative Turks were uneasy, and called Mahmud 'the Infidel Sultan'. Meanwhile, in the West, Turkish

baths and Orientalist paintings were the height of fashion, and the truly chic retired after dinner to luxurious Turkish smoking rooms. It was a courtship of mutual fascination, but with ominous political undercurrents of Western imperialist aspirations.

Turkey was an eager participant in world trade exhibitions. At the Paris Universal Exhibition in 1867, Abdulaziz, the first Ottoman Sultan to pay a state visit abroad, was welcomed with all the honours due to the leader of one of the great world powers. When he reached London from Paris, the streets were lined with cheering crowds, for Britain still remembered her gallant ally of the Crimean War. He arrived on a white charger, a diamond aigrette on his fez, to dine at the Guildhall.

In 1869 Empress Eugénie visited Constantinople on her way to open the Suez Canal. Every item of her dress was scrutinized by invisible eyes. High-heeled shoes replaced Turkish slippers, skirts were favoured over *shalwar* (harem pants), and Sultanas demanded to be dressed by Eugénie's couturier Worth. Pierre Loti resented the intrusion of European fashions into Turkish traditional life, and wrote with disgust of 'those boulevard idlers whom the Orient Express unloads…in hordes.' But the richness of the city comes from its heady mixture of people and styles, filtered through its Ottoman past.

By the late nineteenth century, the Russian railways stretched east, and it was to Turkish Central Asia that Bakst and Diaghilev turned for the vivid silks that amazed the world when their Ballets Russes arrived in Paris in 1909. And it was partly the Turkish tones in the ballet music of Russian composers that entranced Western ears. Throughout the 1920s Matisse painted his series of languid odalisques, and with the advent of cinema, Western ideas of harems embodied fantasies beyond the imaginings of Sheherezade.

The Russian Revolution of 1917 brought refugees to Constantinople, and in the twenties and thirties Pera Palas bar simmered with espionage and clandestine meetings, its walls heard terrible secrets, and the little gilded birdcage lift carried mysterious White Russian Countesses to secret assignations.

Today the bazaars are still redolent with spices, piled with carpets, and gleaming with jewels and silks from every corner of what was once the Ottoman Empire. Old palaces are now museums, thronged by international visitors, who sleep and eat in other palaces which have been transformed into hotels. When the Topkapi's doors close at night, the Lord of the Djinns holds court once more in the palace gardens.

ACKNOWLEDGMENTS

My love and thanks are due to the main cornerstones of my life –
my mother Irene Gillam, and my daughter Chloe Franses.
My thanks, too, to Lord and Lady John Scott, John and Peggy Carswell,
Anne Engel, Kasmin, Naz and Azmet Jah, Ilhan Nebioglu,
Dyala Salam, Richard Trescott, Simon Trewin.

PHOTOGRAPHIC CREDITS

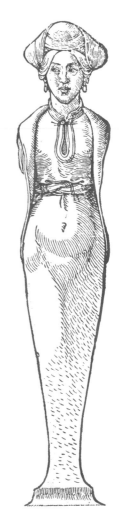

GUIDE

All across Turkey there are fabulous things to be seen, and all over

the world there are museums and collections of Ottoman,

or Ottoman-inspired, art. Here is a selection.

MUSEUMS

ISTANBUL

(always check opening times)

CALLIGRAPHY MUSEUM
Beyazit Square
The only calligraphy museum in the world.

CARPET AND KILIM MUSEUM
Sultanahmet (next to the Blue Mosque)
Until these carpets were collected from mosques all round Turkey, unscrupulous traders and collectors of many different nationalities went round like the sorcerer in the tale of Aladdin, offering new rugs for old.

DIVAN LITERATURE MUSEUM,
(also called the Galata Mevlevihane)
Beyoglu
Collection of musical instruments and dervish items. Whirling Dervishes perform on the last Sunday of every month.

HAGHIA SOPHIA
Sultanahmet
The Church of Holy Wisdom, built by Emperor Justinian *c.* 535 AD, transformed into a mosque after the Ottoman conquest of the city in 1453.

MARITIME MUSEUM
Besiktas
Includes some of the extraordinary boats in which Sultans were rowed along the Bosphorus.

MILITARY MUSEUM
Has wonderful embroidered tents. The Janissary Band performs in the summer, between 3 and 4pm.

RAHMI KOC INDUSTRIAL MUSEUM
Golden Horn
Includes scale models.

SADBERK HANIM MUSEUM
Sariyer
Started as a private collection of domestic items and dress, displayed in a traditional mansion. Now includes archaeological and ethnographical collections.

TOPKAPI SARAYI MUSEUM
Sultanahmet
Breathtaking treasures of the Sultans, including royal kaftans, jewels, the largest collection of Chinese porcelain outside China. Don't miss the Treasury. A separate ticket must be purchased to visit the Harem. Reserve a window seat in the restaurant for a Sultan's eye view of the Bosphorus. The Archaeological Museum is in the palace grounds, to be viewed separately.

TURKISH AND ISLAMIC ART MUSEUM
Ibrahim Pasha Sarayi
Sultanahmet
Includes unique Seljuk and Ottoman carpets, wood, metalwork, ceramics.

AUSTRIA

KUNSTHISTORISCHES MUSEUM
(Kunstkammer)
Vienna

DENMARK

THE DAVID COLLECTION
Copenhagen
Collection includes a unique Iznik vessel known as the 'Mae West jug', a reference to the red 'lips' which pattern it (cf. Salvador Dali's 'Mae West' settee).

FRANCE

MUSÉE DE LA RENAISSANCE
Château d'Ecouen (north of Paris)
In the mid-nineteenth century some five hundred and thirty pieces of Iznik pottery were acquired for the Musée Cluny by the French Consul to the island of Rhodes. Because of this, confusingly, the term 'Rhodian' was often applied to Iznik. This collection is now housed in the Château d'Ecouen.

MUSÉE DU LOUVRE
Paris
Islamic Department includes important Turkish holdings.

MUSÉES HISTORIQUE DES TISSUS
Lyons
Important textile collection includes imperial Ottoman silks woven in the court *ateliers* in Istanbul and Bursa.

GERMANY

MUSEUM FÜR ISLAMISCHE KUNST
Berlin
The Museum's Ottoman holdings include some extremely important rugs and carpets.

STAATLICHEN KUNSTSAMMLUNGEN
Dresden
A stunning collection of Ottoman art and European items 'à la turque'.

BAYERISCHES ARMEEMUSEUM
Ingolstadt
Includes a rare type of Ottoman tent. (see pages 52–53)

LANDESMUSEUM
Karlsruhe
Includes extensive collection from the Turkish Room of Margrave Ludwig Wilhelm von Baden-Baden, nicknamed 'Turkish Louis'.

GREECE

BENAKI MUSEUM
Athens
Ottoman ceramics and textiles include superb Turkish and Greek Island embroideries.

HUNGARY

HUNGARIAN NATIONAL MUSEUM
and MUSEUM OF DECORATIVE ARTS
Budapest
Both conserve sixteenth- and seventeenth-century Turkish rugs and other items.

POLAND

NATIONAL MUSEUM
Warsaw

NATIONAL MUSEUM
Cracow

Both museums and some royal castles hold rich collections of Ottoman art, including horse trappings, weapons, rugs, tents. A loan exhibition of these was shown in the Turkish and Islamic Museum, Istanbul, in 1999.

SWEDEN

CELSING COLLECTION
Uppsala Univesity
Manuscripts and paintings brought back by Ulrik Celsing, Ambassador to the Ottoman court, in the eighteenth century.

SWITZERLAND

MUSÉES D'ART ET D'HISTOIRE
Geneva
The largest collection of paintings and drawings of Europeans in Ottoman dress, by the Swiss artist Liotard, known as 'the Turk'.

UNITED KINGDOM

BRITISH MUSEUM
London
The largest collection of Iznik pottery in the world, though Turkey, of course, has the most important tiles, still *in situ*.

VICTORIA AND ALBERT MUSEUM
London
Amongst its extensive Turkish holdings are several imperial kaftans, including those made for royal children.

ROYAL MUSEUM OF SCOTLAND
Edinburgh
Turkish textiles and items of dress, including a good collection of eighteenth-century Ottoman women's and children's costumes.

Among other museums and galleries in the UK that have good collections of Ottoman textiles (including Algerian and Greek Island embroideries), ceramics, rugs, etc., are:

ASHMOLEAN MUSEUM
Oxford

WHITWORTH GALLERY AND ART MUSEUMS
Manchester

FITZWILLIAM MUSEUM,
Cambridge

UNITED STATES OF AMERICA

COUNTY MUSEUM OF ART
5905 Wilshire Boulevard
Los Angeles CA 90038

ART INSTITUTE OF CHICAGO
Michigan Avenue at Adams Street,
Chicago IL 60603–60110

DE YOUNG MUSEUM
San Francisco CA 94118 4598
Several extensive and important collections of rugs and *kilims*.

TEXTILE MUSEUM
2320 South Street
Washington DC 20008
The first textile purchase of what was destined to become this important museum was an Ottoman domestic embroidery. Includes carpets.

METROPOLITAN MUSEUM OF ART
Fifth Avenue at 82nd
New York NY 10028
The museum's Islamic holdings include important Ottoman art.

MUSEUM OF FINE ARTS
465 Huntington Avenue
Boston MA 02115

BOOKSHOPS
for visitors to Istanbul

GALERI KAYSERI
Divanyolu Cad. 58
Sultanahmet
email: galerikayseri@ihlas.net.tr

ROBINSON CRUSOE
Istiklal Cad. 389
Beyoglu

OTTOMANIA
Eren Ltd. Sti, Tunel
Sofyali Sok. 30–32
Beyoglu
Old maps, engravings and rare books

HOW TO START COLLECTING

• Develop your taste and discover what you really like.
• Museums are vital, but their policy is 'look but don't touch'. In order to handle items, view auctions, and make friends with dealers and ask questions.
• Ask your local museum or auctioneer for the address of your nearest rug, textile, glass or ceramic society, and meet people with similar interests through lectures and meetings.

• Subscribe to the specialist magazines *Hali* and *Cornucopia*, or ask your local library to subscribe, as neither has newstand outlets. *Cornucopia* , published in English three times a year, covers Turkish history, art, culture, present and future. Contact at:
PO Box 13311, Hawick TD9 7YF, Scotland;
PO Box 3405, Sunriver, OR 97707, USA;
CC480 Mecidiyekoy, 80303, Istanbul, Turkey;
Hali, published six times a year, specializes in carpets, textiles, Asian and Islamic art:
email: hali@subscription.co.uk
• Go to antiques fairs and look closely.
• Eventually you will discover the dealers whose tastes reflect your own. Outside Turkey, it is rare to find a dealer who specializes only in Turkish art.
• Depending on what you want, it is sometimes better to buy in Turkey, and sometimes better to buy abroad.
• Islamic auctions in London:
Spring and autumn, during 'Islamic Week', Sotheby's, Christie's and Bonham's hold specialist sales.
In June every year, Christie's usually hold an Ottoman and Orientalists sale.
London and New York auction houses have Islamic Departments.
Islamic auctions in Paris:
Paris auction houses employ freelance consultants. Auctions are held at the Hôtel Drouot. The main Parisian auctioneers for Turkish art and Orientalist paintings are:
Etude Tajan (consultant Lucien Arcache);
Gros Delettrez, and François de Ricqles (consultants Lynne Thornton and Cabinet Soustiel-David);
Claude Boisgirard (consultant A. M. Kevorkian).
There are sales of works of art, furniture, pictures, manuscripts, miniatures, textiles,

rugs, jewelry, ceramics, glass, silver, arms and armour, accompanied by informative illustrated catalogues.
• Orientalist pictures with Turkish scenes can also be found in sales of nineteenth-century paintings.

WHAT TO COLLECT

If space is a problem: small rugs; woven bags; spoons made of tortoiseshell, coconut shell, bone, ivory, mother-of-pearl, ebony, and with handles tipped with coral; glass rosewater sprinklers; *hamam* items; coffee cups; embroidered scarves. Or select an Orientalist painting, and look for items similar to those the artist has used as studio props. Even fragments of embroidery can look beautiful, mounted and displayed, but not in direct light, because it destroys and fades fabrics over time.

WHERE TO BUY

IN TURKEY

CERAMICS

There are some outstanding contemporary ceramicists working in the tradition of Iznik and Kutahya. Their work can be bought at source, in various commercial outlets in Istanbul, and at the shop in the Museum of Turkish and Islamic Art (see above). The best of these are the heirlooms of tomorrow.

ISMAIL YIGIT

Valikonagi Cad. Ekmek Fabrikasi Sok
2/16 Nisantasi
Istanbul
Tel. +90-212-233 3322
and also at
Ataturk Bulvari 39/A
Kutahya
Istanbul
Traditional Ottoman Iznik and Kutahya pottery, superb quality, exported and sold in such outlets as the Victoria & Albert Museum shop in London.

THE IZNIK FOUNDATION

Iznik Cini ve Seramik Isletmesi
Kurucesme
Oksuz Cocuk Sk. no 14 Besiktas
Istanbul
www.iznik.com
Specializes in tiles, and supplied those decorating the walls of Istanbul's first Metro stations (system opened 2000) and many

corporate buildings. Will ship abroad. You can visit their *ateliers* in the town of Iznik, and also the Istanbul showroom.

IZNIK CLASSICS

Old Bazaar and also at
Arasta Carsisi no. 67
Sultanahmet
Istanbul
Ceramics from various potters, including the above.

CARPETS AND TEXTILES

An interesting effect of the Soviet Union's break-up has been the rapprochement of Turkic Central Asia with Turkey, and there are many Turkoman carpets and textiles among the Turkish, Kurdish, Caucasian and other weavings.
The only way to choose a carpet is to buy what you really like, and spend time looking. Enjoy the process and the tea or coffee which accompanies it. Modern Turkish carpets are, on the whole, good quality, and, although carpet dealers are famous for their persuasive powers, bazaar badinage is good humoured. There is no reason for the experience to be other than positive.

GUNES OZTARAKCI

Mim Kemal Oke Cad. 5
Nisantasi
Istanbul
By appointment only
Tel. +90-212 225 1954
A successful woman in the male-dominated world of carpet trading.

A LA TURCA
Faikpasa Yokusu no. 4 Cukurcuma
Cihangir
Istanbul
Tel/Fax. +90-212 245 29 33

OTTOMANIA
Takkeciler Sokak
78–80 Grand Bazaar
Istanbul
Tel. +90-212 527 9308

VAKKO
123–25 Istiklal Cad.
Istanbul
Of the modern textile firms reproducing
Ottoman patterns, the best known is
Vakko, whose several outlets include
a large showroom on Istiklal Cad.
They make both furnishing and
fashion fabrics.

KUSAV
(Foundation for the Conservation
and Promotion of Culture and Arts).
Contact on Tel. +90 212 262 34 33 09 86
For antique carpet auctions, held
every other Sunday, and antique
and decorative arts fairs.

WHERE TO BUY

ABROAD

'By appointment only' means that this
is not a gallery you can walk into, or
even find by walking down a street.
Unlike national museums, private
sources change location, or change
focus depending on market interest,
and of course people retire and
close their businesses.

AUSTRALIA
ANN AND GEOFFREY LONG
Gaanetgetal Books
23 Fowler Street
Camperdown
NSW 2050

ORIENTAL RUG SOCIETY
OF NEW SOUTH WALES
PO Box 56
Surry Hills
NSW 2010

ROSS LANGLAND
Nomadic Rugs
125 Harris Street
Pyrmont

Sydney
NSW 2009

KERRY AND PAM HOYNE
Gallery Dobag
131 Bussell Highway
Margaret River
Western Australia 6288

CITO CESSNA
Enshallah Trading Co.
21 Barwun Road
Lane Cove
NSW 2066

FRANCE
BERDJ ACHDJIAN
10 Rue de Miromesnil
75008 Paris
Tel. +33 (0) 1 42 65 89 48
Long-established family firm
dealing in classic rugs and carpets,
especially antique Caucasians.

GALERIE J. SOUSTIEL
146 Boulevard Haussmann
75008 Paris
Tel. +33 (0) 1 45 63 48 22
Several generations specializing in
Islamic and Ottoman works of art.

GALERIE TRIFF
35 Rue Jacob
75000 Paris
Tel +33 (0) 1 42 60 22 60
Antique Turkish rugs and *kilims*.

GALERIE KEVORKIAN
21 Quai Malaquais
75006 Paris
Tel. +33 (0) 1 42 60 72 91
Islamic works of art,
including Ottoman.

GERMANY
OTTOMANIA
Fedelhoren 102
28209 Bremen

ITALY
ALBERTO BORALEVI
Via Monalda 15/r
50123 Florence
tel. +39 (0) 55 211 423
Classic carpets and textiles
fit for any palazzo.

OTTOMAN ART
Via Della Sposa 10 & 15
06123 Perugia
Tel. +39 (0) 75 573 6842

UNITED KINGDOM

BRENDON LYNCH AND
OLIVER FORGE
Flat 2
10 Bury Street
London SW1Y 6AA
Tel. +44 (0) 20 7829 0368
Indian and Islamic Art.

FRANCESCA GALLOWAY
21 Cornwall Gardens
London SW7 4AW
By appointment only –
Tel. +44 (0)20 7937 3192
Costumes, textiles, Islamic art
and miniatures.

MOMTAZ ISLAMIC ART
79A Albany Street
Regent's Park
By appointment only
Tel. +44 (0) 20 7486 5411

DYALA SALAM
174A Kensington Church Street
London W8 4DP
Tel.+44 (0)20 7229 4045
The prettiest shop in London, decorated
like the Fruit Room in the Topkapi Sarayi,
London's specialist in *turqueries.*

SPINK INDIAN & ISLAMIC WORKS OF ART
21 King Street
St James's
London SW1Y 6QY
Tel +44 (0) 20 7930 5500

MICHAEL AND HENRIETTA SPINK
3 Georgian House
10 Bury Street
London SW1Y 6AA

Tel. +44(0)20 7930 2288
Indian and Islamic Art.

In London, for those who want to create
a Turkish interior, first stop must be
Dyala Salam (see above), then browse
in the antique shops in Pimlico and
along New Kings Road, many of whom
will have mother-of-pearl inlaid mirrors,
little tables, and furniture from the
Ottoman empire.

UNITED STATES OF AMERICA

JAMES BLACKMON
2140 Bush Street, no. 1
San Francisco, CA 94115
Tel. +1-415 922 1859

CARAVANSERAI LTD.
Casey Waller
1435 Dragon Street
Dallas, TX 75207
Tel. +1-214 741 2131
Superb textiles from Turkestan

DENNIS R. DODDS
Maqam
PO Box 4312
Philadelphia, PA 19118
Tel. +1-215 247 4774

J.H. TERRY
313A 1st Avenue South
Seattle, WA 98104
Tel. +1-206 233 9766

SELECT BIBLIOGRAPHY

Barillari, Diana, and Ezio Godoli,
Istanbul 1900, New York, 1996
Batari, Ferenc, *Ottoman Turkish
Carpets*, Budapest, 1994
Blanch, Lesley, *Pierre Loti*,
London, 1983
Bradford, Ernie, *The Sultan's
Admiral: The Life of Barbarossa*,
London, 1968
Bon, Ottavio, and Godfrey Goodwin,
The Sultan's Seraglio,
London, 1996
Carswell, John, *Iznik Pottery*,
London, 1998
Carswell, John, 'Order of the Bath
(Ingres and Lady Mary Wortley-
Montagu)', *Cornucopia*,
Issue 10, Vol. II, 1996
Cassels, Lavender, *The Struggle for
the Ottoman Empire 1717–1740*,
London and New York, 1966
Chew, Samuel, *The Crescent and the
Rose*, London and New York, 1937
Clot, André, *Soliman le Magnifique*,
Paris, 1980
Coles, Paul, *The Ottoman Impact
on Europe*, London and
New York, 1968

Corti, Count, *A History of Smoking*,
London, 1931
Cuddon, J. A., *The Owl's Watchsong*,
London and New York, 1960
Croutier, Alev Lytle, *Harem:
The World behind the Veil*,
New York, 1989
Dash, Mike, *Tulipomania*,
London and New York, 1999
Ellison, Grace, *An English Woman
in a Turkish Harem*, London, 1915
Erdman, Kurt, *The History of the
Early Turkish Carpet*,
London, 1977
Erdogan, Sema Nilgun, *Sexual Life in
Ottoman Society*, Istanbul, 1996
Freely, John, *Inside the Seraglio:
Private Lives of the Sultans in
Istanbul*, London, 1999
Freely, John, *Istanbul, the Imperial
City*, London, 1996;
New York, 1998
Gervers, Veronika, *The Influence
of Ottoman Turkish Textiles and
Costume in Eastern Europe*,
Ontario, 1982
Gocek, Fatma Muge, *East Encounters
West*, Oxford, 1987

Goodwin, Godfrey, *A History of
Ottoman Architecture*, London, 1971
Goodwin, Godfrey, *The Janissaries*,
London, 1994
Goodwin, Godfrey, *The Private
World of Ottoman Women,*
London, 1997
Goodwin, Godfrey, *The Topkapi
Palace*, London, 1999
Grundy, Isobel, *Lady Mary Wortley
Montagu, Comet of the
Enlightenment*, Oxford, 1900
Hanimefendi, Leyla, *Le Harem
Imperial*, Paris, 1925
Hattox, Ralph, *Coffee and Coffee
Houses*, Washington, 1985
Hellier, Chris and Francisco Venturi,
Splendours of the Bosphorus,
London, 1993
Inalcik, Halil, *An Economic and Social
History of the Ottoman Empire,
1300–1914,* 2 vols, Cambridge, 1994
Inalcik, Halil, *The Ottoman Empire:
The Classical Age 1300–1600*,
London and New York, 1973
Jardine, Lisa, *Worldly Goods:
A New History of the Renaissance*,
London and New York, 1996

Lane-Poole, Stanley, *The Barbary Corsairs*, London, 1890; Westport, Conn., 1970

Loti, Pierre, *Aziyadé*, Paris, (first published 1879), 1927

Lloyd, Christopher, *English Corsairs on the Barbary Coast*, London, 1981

McKenzie, John, *Orientalism: History, Theory and the Arts*, Manchester and New York, 1995

Mansel, Philip, *Constantinople: City of the World's Desire*, London, 1995; New York, 1996

Montagu-Wortley, Lady Mary, *The Turkish Embassy Letters*, London 1763; edited by M. Jack, Athens, Georgia, 1993

Murad, Kenize, *Farewell Princess*, London, 1990

Orga, Irfan, *Portrait of a Turkish Family*, London, 1950; New York, 1988

Oz, Tahsin, *Turkish Textiles and Velvets XIV–XVI Centuries*, Ankara, 1950

Pavord, Anna, *The Tulip*, London, 1999

Penzer, N. M., *The Harem*, London, 1936

Peirce, Leslie, *The Imperial Harem*, Oxford, 1993

Porter, Venetia, *Islamic Tiles*, London and New York, 1995

Raby, Julian, *Venice, Dürer and the Oriental Mode*, London, 1982

Roden, Claudia, *Coffee*, London, 1977

Runciman, Steven, *The Fall of Constantinople 1453*, Cambridge, 1965

Scarce, Jennifer, *Women's Costume of the Near and Middle East*, London, 1987

Schwoebel, Robert, *Shadow of the Crescent*, New York, 1967

Scott, Philippa, *The Book of Silk*, London and New York, 1993

Sumner-Boyd, Hilary, and John Freely, *Strolling Through Istanbul: A Guide to the City*, London, 1972; New York, 1987

Sweetman, John, *The Oriental Obsession*, Cambridge, 1987

Tezcan, Hulye, and Selma Delibas, (trans. J. M. Rogers), *The Topkapi Sarayi Museum: Textiles*, London and New York, 1986

Ther, Ulla, *Floral Messages*, Bremen, 1993

Wheatcroft, Andrew, *The Ottomans*, London, 1993

Ydema, Onno, *Carpets and their Datings in Netherlandish Paintings 1540–1700*, Leiden, 1991

Yerasimos, Stephane, Ara Guler and Samih Rifat, *Living in Turkey*, London, 1992; New York, 2001

EXHIBITION CATALOGUES

Albertinum, *In Liche des Halmonds*, Staatliche Kunstammlungen, Dresden, 1995

Altonaer Museum, *A Wealth of Silk and Velvet*, Hamburg, 1993

Brunei Gallery, *Empire of the Sultans*, London, 1996

Château de Versailles, *Topkapi à Versailles*, Paris, 1999

Centre Culturel Boulogne-Billancourt, *Au Nom de la Tulipe*, Paris, 1993

Colnaghi, *Imperial Ottoman Textiles*, London, 1980

Corcoran Gallery of Art, *Palace of Gold and Light*, Washington, DC, 2000

David Black, *Embroidered Flowers from Thrace to Tartary*, London, 1981

David Collection, *By the Light of the Crescent Moon*, Copenhagen, 1996

National Gallery of Art (Esin Atil), *The Age of Suleiman the Magnificent*, Washington, DC, 1987

Hazlitt Gooden & Fox Gallery, *At the Sublime Porte*, London, 1988

Hayward Gallery, *The Arts of Islam*, London, 1976

Hayward Gallery, *The Eastern Carpet in the Western World from the 15th to the 17th Century*, London, 1983

Kyburg Gallery, (E. Grunberg and E. Torn, eds), *Four Centuries of Ottoman Taste*, London, 1988

National Gallery of Ireland, *The East Imagined, Experienced, Remembered*, Dublin, 1988

National Museum, *Sultan, Shah and Great Mughal*, Copenhagen, 1996

Royal Academy of Arts, *The Orientalists: From Delacroix to Matisse*, London, 1984

Scottish National Portrait Gallery, *Visions of the Ottoman Empire*, Edinburgh, 1994

Spink, *Visions of the Orient*, London, 1995

Textile Museum, *The Splendor of Turkish Weaving*, Washington, DC, 1973

Textile Museum, *Flowers of Silk and Gold*, Washington, DC, 2000

Topkapi Sarayi Museum, *9000 Years of the Anatolian Woman*, Istanbul, 1993

PAGE 113: Design for a ewer, etching by
Wenzel Hollar after Hans Holbein, 1645.
PAGES 114 AND 117: details from Albrecht
Dürer's *The Turkish Family*, engraving
1497/1500. PAGE 115: Drawing of a
17th-century money token for use in
an English coffee-house, British Museum.
PAGE 116 LEFT: Ornamental arabesque
border, woodcut from G. A. Tagliente,
Opera nuova..., Venice, 1530.
PAGES 116 RIGHT AND 119: Ottoman
costumes from *Descriptions de l'Egypte*,
Paris, 1822–23. PAGE 120: Calligraphic
drawing of peacocks holding open books,
Turkish, 1890, private collection.